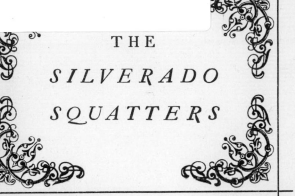

THE
SILVERADO
SQUATTERS

By Robert Louis Stevenson, 1850-1894.

San Francisco:
The Grabhorn Press
McMLII.

TO

Virgil Williams

AND

Dora Norton Williams

THESE SKETCHES

ARE AFFECTIONATELY DEDICATED

BY THEIR FRIEND

THE AUTHOR

CONTENTS

"*Vixerunt nonulli in agris, delectati re sua familiari. His idem propositum fuit quod regibus, ut ne qua re agerent, ne cui parerent, libertate uterentur: cujus proprium est sic vivere ut velis.*"

—Cic., *De Off.*, I. xx.

THIS BOOK REPRINTED FROM THE FIRST EDITION
PUBLISHED BY CHATTO & WINDUS, LONDON, 1883.

THE SILVERADO SQUATTERS.

THE SILVERADO
SQUATTERS

THE SCENE of this little book is on a high mountain. There are, indeed, many higher; there are many of a nobler outline. It is no place of pilgrimage for the summary globe-trotter; but to one who lives upon its sides, Mount Saint Helena soon becomes a centre of interest. It is the Mont Blanc of one section of the Californian Coast Range, none of its near neighbours rising to one-half its altitude. It looks down on much green, intricate country. It feeds in the springtime many splashing brooks. From its summit you must have an excellent lesson of geography: seeing, to the south, San Francisco Bay,

with Tamalpais on the one hand and Monte
Diablo on the other; to the west and thirty miles
away, the open ocean; eastward, across the corn-
lands and thick tule swamps of Sacramento
Valley, to where the Central Pacific railroad be-
gins to climb the sides of the Sierras; and northward, for what I know, the white head of Shas-
ta looking down on Oregon. Three counties,
Napa County, Lake County, and Sonoma County, march across its cliffy shoulders. Its naked
peak stands nearly four thousand five hundred
feet above the sea; its sides are fringed with
forest; and the soil, where it is bare, glows
warm with cinnabar.

Life in its shadow goes rustically forward.
Bucks, and bears, and rattlesnakes, and former
mining operations, are the staple of men's talk.
Agriculture has only begun to mount above the
valley. And though in a few years from now
the whole district may be smiling with farms,
passing trains shaking the mountain to the
heart, many-windowed hotels lighting up the
night like factories, and a prosperous city oc-

cupying the site of sleepy Calistoga; yet in the mean time, around the foot of that mountain the silence of nature reigns in a great measure unbroken, and the people of hill and valley go sauntering about their business as in the days before the flood.

To reach Mount Saint Helena from San Francisco, the traveller has twice to cross the bay: once by the busy Oakland Ferry, and again, after an hour or so of the railway, from Vallejo junction to Vallejo. Thence he takes rail once more to mount the long green strath of Napa Valley.

In all the contractions and expansions of that inland sea, the Bay of San Francisco, there can be few drearier scenes than the Vallejo Ferry. Bald shores and a low, bald islet inclose the sea; through the narrows the tide bubbles, muddy like a river. When we made the passage (bound, although yet we knew it not, for Silverado) the steamer jumped, and the black buoys were dancing in the jabble; the ocean breeze blew killing chill; and, although the upper sky was still unflecked with vapour, the sea fogs were pouring in from seaward, over the hilltops of Marin County, in one great, shapeless, silver cloud.

South Vallejo is typical of many Californian towns. It was a blunder; the site proved untenable; and, although it is still such a young place by the scale of Europe, it has already begun to be deserted for its neighbour and namesake, North Vallejo. A long pier, a number of drinking saloons, a hotel of a great size, marshy pools where the frogs keep up their croaking, and even at high noon the entire absence of any human face or voice—these are the marks of South Vallejo. Yet there was a tall building beside the pier, labelled the *Star Flour Mills;* and sea-going, full-rigged ships lay close along shore, waiting for their cargo. Soon these would be plunging round the Horn, soon the flour from the *Star Flour Mills* would be landed on the wharves of Liverpool. For that, too, is one of England's outposts; thither, to this gaunt mill, across the Atlantic and Pacific deeps and round about the icy Horn, this crowd of great, three-

masted, deep-sea ships come, bringing nothing,
and return with bread.

The Frisby House, for that was the name of
the hotel, was a place of fallen fortunes, like the
town. It was now given up to labourers, and
partly ruinous. At dinner there was the ordinary
display of what is called in the west a *two-bit
house:* the tablecloth checked red and white, the
plague of flies, the wire hencoops over the dishes, the great variety and invariable vileness of
the food, and the rough coatless men devouring
it in silence. In our bedroom, the stove would
not burn, though it would smoke; and while
one window would not open, the other would
not shut. There was a view on a bit of empty
road, a few dark houses, a donkey wandering
with its shadow on a slope, and a blink of sea,
with a tall ship lying anchored in the moonlight. All about that dreary inn frogs sang their
ungainly chorus.

Early the next morning we mounted the hill
along a wooden footway, bridging one marish
spot after another. Here and there, as we as-

cended, we passed a house embowered in white roses. More of the bay became apparent, and soon the blue peak of Tamalpais rose above the green level of the island opposite. It told us we were still but a little way from the city of the Golden Gates, already, at that hour, beginning to awake among the sand-hills. It called to us over the waters as with the voice of a bird. Its stately head, blue as a sapphire on the paler azure of the sky, spoke to us of wider outlooks and the bright Pacific. For Tamalpais stands sentry, like a lighthouse, over the Golden Gates, between the bay and the open ocean, and looks down indifferently on both. Even as we saw and hailed it from Vallejo, seamen, far out at sea, were scanning it with shaded eyes; and, as if to answer to the thought, one of the great ships below began silently to clothe herself with white sails, homeward bound for England.

For some way beyond Vallejo the railway led us through bald green pastures. On the west the rough highlands of Marin shut off the ocean; in the midst, in long, straggling, gleaming arms, the bay died out among the grass; there were few trees and few enclosures; the sun shone wide over open uplands, the displumed hills stood clear against the sky. But by-and-by these hills began to draw nearer on either hand, and first thicket and then wood began to clothe their sides; and soon we were away from all signs of the sea's neighborhood, mounting an inland, irrigated valley. A great variety of oaks stood, now severally, now in a becoming grove, among the fields and vineyards. The towns were compact, in about equal proportions, of bright, new wooden houses and great and growing forest trees; and the chapel bell on the engine sounded most festally that sunny Sunday, as we drew up at one green town after another, with the townsfolk trooping in their Sunday's best to see the strangers, with the sun sparkling on the clean houses, and great domes of foliage humming overhead in the breeze.

This pleasant Napa Valley is, at its north end, blockaded by our mountain. There, at Calistoga, the railroad ceases, and the traveller who intends faring farther, to the Geysers or to the springs in Lake County, must cross the spurs of the mountain by stage. Thus, Mount Saint Helena is not only a summit, but a frontier; and, up to the time of writing, it has stayed the progress of the iron horse.

IN THE VALLEY

I.

CALISTOGA

IT IS DIFFICULT for a European to imagine Calistoga, the whole place is so new, and of such an occidental pattern; the very name, I hear, was invented at a supper-party by the man who found the springs.

The railroad and the highway come up the valley about parallel to one another. The street of Calistoga joins them, perpendicular to both— a wide street, with bright, clean, low houses, here and there a verandah over the sidewalk, here and there a horse-post, here and there lounging townsfolk. Other streets are marked out, and most likely named; for these towns in the

New World begin with a firm resolve to grow
larger, Washington and Broadway, and then
First and Second, and so forth, being boldly
plotted out as soon as the community indulges
in a plan. But, in the meanwhile, all the life and
most of the houses of Calistoga are concentrated
upon that street between the railway station and
the road. I never heard it called by any name,
but I will hazard a guess that it is either Washington or Broadway. Here are the blacksmith's,
the chemist's, the general merchant's, and
Kong Sam Kee, the Chinese laundry man's;
here, probably, is the office of the local paper
(for the place has a paper—they all have papers);
and here certainly is one of the hotels, Cheeseborough's, whence the daring Foss, a man dear
to legend, starts his horses for the Geysers.

It must be remembered that we are here in a
land of stage-drivers and highwaymen: a land,
in that sense, like England a hundred years ago.
The highway robber—road-agent, he is quaint-
ly called—is still busy in these parts. The fame
of Vasquez is still young. Only a few years ago,

the Lakeport stage was robbed a mile or two
from Calistoga. In 1879, the dentist of Mendocino City, fifty miles away upon the coast, suddenly threw off the garments of his trade, like
Grindoff, in *The Miller and his Men*, and flamed
forth in his second dress as a captain of ban-
ditti. A great robbery was followed by a long
chase, a chase of days if not of weeks, among
the intricate hill country; and the chase was followed by much desultory fighting, in which
several — and the dentist, I believe, amongst
the number—bit the dust. The grass was springing for the first time, nourished upon their blood,
when I arrived in Calistoga. I am reminded of
another highwayman of that same year. "He
had been unwell," so ran his humorous defence,
"and the doctor told him to take something,
so he took the express-box."

The cultus of the stage-coachman always
flourishes highest where there are thieves on the
road, and where the guard travels armed, and
the stage is not only a link between country and
city, and the vehicle of news, but has a faint

warfaring aroma, like a man who should be brother to a soldier. California boasts her famous stage-drivers, and among the famous Foss is not forgotten. Along the unfenced, abominable mountain roads, he launches his team with small regard to human life or the doctrine of probabilities. Flinching travellers, who behold themselves coasting eternity at every corner, look with natural admiration at their driver's huge, impassive, fleshy countenance. He has the very face for the driver in Sam Weller's anecdote, who upset the election party at the required point. Wonderful tales are current of his readiness and skill. One in particular, of how one of his horses fell at a ticklish passage of the road, and how Foss let slip the reins, and, driving over the fallen animal, arrived at the next stage with only three. This I relate as I heard it, without guarantee.

I only saw Foss once, though, strange as it may sound, I have twice talked with him. He lives out of Calistoga, at a ranche called Fossville. One evening, after he was long gone home,

In the Valley

I dropped into Cheeseborough's, and was asked
if I should like to speak with Mr. Foss. Sup-
posing that the interview was impossible, and
that I was merely called upon to subscribe the
general sentiment, I boldly answered "Yes."
Next moment, I had one instrument at my ear,
another at my mouth, and found myself, with
nothing in the world to say, conversing with a
man several miles off among desolate hills. Foss
rapidly and somewhat plaintively brought the
conversation to an end; and he returned to his
night's grog at Fossville, while I strolled forth
again on Calistoga high street. But it was an
odd thing that here, on what we are accustomed
to consider the very skirts of civilization, I
should have used the telephone for the first time
in my civilized career. So it goes in these young
countries; telephones, and telegraphs, and newspapers, and advertisements running far ahead
among the Indians and the grizzly bears.

Alone, on the other side of the railway, stands
the Springs Hotel, with its attendant cottages.
The floor of the valley is extremely level to the

very roots of the hills; only here and there a
hillock, crowned with pines, rises like the bar-
row of some chieftain famed in war; and right
against one of these hillocks is the Springs Hotel—is or was; for since I was there the place
has been destroyed by fire, and has risen again
from its ashes. A lawn runs about the house,
and the lawn is in its turn surrounded by a sys-
tem of little five-roomed cottages, each with a
verandah and a weedy palm before the door.
Some of the cottages are let to residents, and
these are wreathed in flowers. The rest are occupied by ordinary visitors to the hotel; and a
very pleasant way this is, by which you have
a little country cottage of your own, without
domestic burthens, and by the day or week.

The whole neighbourhood of Mount Saint
Helena is full of sulphur and of boiling springs.
The Geysers are famous; they were the great
health resort of the Indians before the coming
of the whites. Lake County is dotted with spas;
Hot Springs and White Sulphur Springs are
the names of two stations on the Napa Valley

railroad; and Calistoga itself seems to repose on a mere film above a boiling, subterranean lake. At one end of the hotel enclosure are the springs from which it takes its name, hot enough to scald a child seriously while I was there. At the other end, the tenant of a cottage sank a well, and there also the water came up boiling. It keeps this end of the valley as warm as a toast. I have gone across to the hotel a little after five in the morning, when a sea fog from the Pacific was hanging thick and gray, and dark and dirty overhead, and found the thermometer had been up before me, and had already climbed among the nineties; and in the stress of the day it was sometimes too hot to move about.

But in spite of this heat from above and below, doing one on both sides, Calistoga was a pleasant place to dwell in; beautifully green, for it was then that favoured moment in the Californian year, when the rains are over and the dusty summer has not yet set in; often visited by fresh airs, now from the mountain, now across Sonoma from the sea; very quiet, very

idle, very silent but for the breezes and the cattle
bells afield. And there was something satisfac-
tory in the sight of that great mountain that en-
closed us to the north: whether it stood, robed
in sunshine, quaking to its topmost pinnacle
with the heat and brightness of the day; or
whether it set itself to weaving vapours, wisp
after wisp growing, trembling, fleeting, and
fading in the blue.

The tangled, woody, and almost trackless
foot-hills that enclose the valley, shutting it off
from Sonoma on the west, and from Yolo on the
east—rough as they were in outline, dug out
by winter streams, crowned by cliffy bluffs and
nodding pine trees—were dwarfed into satellites
by the bulk and bearing of Mount Saint Helena.
She over-towered them by two-thirds of her
own stature. She excelled them by the boldness
of her profile. Her great bald summit, clear of
trees and pasture, a cairn of quartz and cinnabar, rejected kinship with the dark and shaggy
wilderness of lesser hill-tops.

II.

The Petrified Forest

WE DROVE OFF from the Springs Hotel about three in the afternoon. The sun warmed me to the heart. A broad, cool wind streamed pauselessly down the valley, laden with perfume. Up at the top stood Mount Saint Helena, a bulk of mountain, bare atop, with tree-fringed spurs, and radiating warmth. Once we saw it framed in a grove of tall and exquisitely graceful white oaks, in line and colour a finished composition. We passed a cow stretched by the roadside, her bell slowly beating time to the movement of her ruminating jaws, her big red face crawled over by half a dozen flies, a monument of content.

A little farther, and we struck to the left up
a mountain road, and for two hours threaded
one valley after another, green, tangled, full of
noble timber, giving us every now and again a
sight of Mount Saint Helena and the blue hilly
distance, and crossed by many streams, through
which we splashed to the carriage-step. To the
right or the left, there was scarce any trace of
man but the road we followed; I think we passed
but one ranchero's house in the whole distance,
and that was closed and smokeless. But we had
the society of these bright streams—dazzlingly
clear, as is their wont, splashing from the wheels
in diamonds, and striking a lively coolness
through the sunshine. And what with the innumerable variety of greens, the masses of foliage tossing in the breeze, the glimpses of distance, the descents into seemingly impenetrable
thickets, the continual dodging of the road
which made haste to plunge again into the covert, we had a fine sense of woods, and springtime, and the open air.

Our driver gave me a lecture by the way on

In the Valley

Californian trees—a thing I was much in need of, having fallen among painters who know the name of nothing, and Mexicans who know the name of nothing in English. He taught me the madrona, the manzanita, the buck-eye, the maple ; he showed me the crested mountain quail; he showed me where some young redwoods were already spiring heavenwards from the ruins of the old; for in this district all had already perished: redwoods and redskins, the two noblest indigenous living things, alike condemned.

At length, in a lonely dell, we came on a huge wooden gate with a sign upon it like an inn. "The Petrified Forest. Proprietor: C. Evans," ran the legend. Within, on a knoll of sward, was the house of the proprietor, and another smaller house hard by to serve as a museum, where photographs and petrifactions were retailed. It was a pure little isle of touristry among these solitary hills.

The proprietor was a brave old white-faced Swede. He had wandered this way, Heaven knows how, and taken up his acres—I forget how many years ago—all alone, bent double with sciatica, and with six bits in his pocket and an axe upon his shoulder. Long, useless years of seafaring had thus discharged him at the end, penniless and sick. Without doubt he had tried his luck at the diggings, and got no good from that; without doubt he had loved the bottle, and lived the life of Jack ashore. But at the end of these adventures, here he came; and, the place hitting his fancy, down he sat to make a new life of it, far from crimps and the salt sea. And the very sight of his ranche had done him good. It was "the handsomest spot in the Californy mountains." "Isn't it handsome, now?" he said. Every penny he makes goes into that ranche to make it handsomer. Then the climate, with the sea-breeze every afternoon in the hottest summer weather, had gradually cured the sciatica; and his sister and niece were now domesticated with him for company—or, rather, the niece came only once in the two days, teaching music the meanwhile in the valley. And

then, for a last piece of luck, "the handsomest
spot in the Californy mountains" had produced
a petrified forest, which Mr. Evans now shows
at the modest figure of half a dollar a head, or
two-thirds of his capital when he first came
there with an axe and a sciatica.

This tardy favourite of fortune—hobbling a
little, I think, as if in memory of the sciatica,
but with not a trace that I can remember of the
sea—thoroughly ruralized from head to foot,
proceeded to escort us up the hill behind his
house.

"Who first found the forest?" asked my wife.

"The first? I was that man," said he. "I was
cleaning up the pasture for my beasts, when I
found *this*"—kicking a great redwood, seven
feet in diameter, that lay there on its side, hollow heart, clinging lumps of bark, all changed
into gray stone, with veins of quartz between
what had been the layers of the wood.

"Were you surprised?"

"Surprised? No! What would I be surprised
about? What did I know about petrifactions—

following the sea? Petrifaction! There was no such word in my language! I knew about putrifaction, though! I thought it was a stone; so would you, if you was cleaning up pasture."

And now he had a theory of his own, which I did not quite grasp, except that the trees had not "grewed" there. But he mentioned, with evident pride, that he differed from all the scientific people who had visited the spot; and he flung about such words as "tufa" and "scilica" with careless freedom.

When I mentioned I was from Scotland, "My old country," he said; "my old country"—with a smiling look and a tone of real affection in his voice. I was mightily surprised, for he was obviously Scandinavian, and begged him to explain. It seemed he had learned his English and done nearly all his sailing in Scotch ships. "Out of Glasgow," said he, "or Greenock; but that's all the same — they all hail from Glasgow." And he was so pleased with me for being a Scotsman, and his adopted compatriot, that he made me a present of a very beautiful piece of petrifaction — I believe the most beautiful and portable he had.

Here was a man, at least, who was a Swede, a Scot, and an American, acknowledging some kind of allegiance to three lands. Mr. Wallace's Scoto-Circassian will not fail to come before the reader. I have myself met and spoke with a Fifeshire German, whose combination of abominable accents struck me dumb. But, indeed, I think we all belong to many countries. And perhaps this habit of much travel, and the engendering of scattered friendships, may prepare the euthanasia of ancient nations.

And the forest itself? Well, on a tangled, briery hillside — for the pasture would bear a little further cleaning up, to my eyes—there lie scattered thickly various lengths of petrified trunk, such as the one already mentioned. It is very curious, of course, and ancient enough, if that were all. Doubtless, the heart of the geologist beats quicker at the sight; but for my part, I was mightily unmoved. Sight-seeing is the art of disappointment.

"There's nothing under heaven so blue,
That's fairly worth the travelling to."

But, fortunately, Heaven rewards us with many agreeable prospects and adventures by the way; and sometimes, when we go out to see a petrified forest, prepares a far more delightful curiosity in the form of Mr. Evans, whom may all prosperity attend throughout a long and green old age.

IN THE VALLEY

III.

NAPA WINE

I WAS INTERESTED in Californian wine. Indeed,
I am interested in all wines, and have been all
my life, from the raisin wine that a schoolfellow
kept secreted in his play-box up to my last discovery, those notable Valtellines, that once
shone upon the board of Cæsar.

Some of us, kind old Pagans, watch with
dread the shadows falling on the age: how the
unconquerable worm invades the sunny ter-
races of France, and Bordeaux is no more, and
the Rhône a mere Arabia Petræa. Château Neuf
is dead, and I have never tasted it; Hermitage—
a hermitage indeed from all life's sorrows—lies

expiring by the river. And in the place of these
imperial elixirs, beautiful to every sense, gem-
hued, flower-scented, dream-compellers: — behold upon the quays at Cette the chemicals ar-
rayed; behold the analyst at Marseilles, raising
hands in obsecration, attesting God Lyœus,
and the vats staved in, and the dishonest wines
poured forth among the sea. It is not Pan only;
Bacchus, too, is dead.

If wine is to withdraw its most poetic countenance, the sun of the white dinner-cloth, a
deity to be invoked by two or three, all fervent,
hushing their talk, degusting tenderly, and
storing reminiscences — for a bottle of good
wine, like a good act, shines ever in the retro-
spect—if wine is to desert us, go thy ways, old
Jack! Now we begin to have compunctions,
and look back at the brave bottles squandered
upon dinner-parties, where the guests drank
grossly, discussing politics the while, and even
the schoolboy "took his whack," like liquorice
water. And at the same time, we look timidly
forward, with a spark of hope, to where the new

lands, already weary of producing gold, begin
to green with vineyards. A nice point in human
history falls to be decided by Californian and
Australian wines.

Wine in California is still in the experimental
stage; and when you taste a vintage, grave eco-
nomical questions are involved. The beginning
of vine-planting is like the beginning of mining for the precious metals: the wine-grower
also "prospects." One corner of land after another is tried with one kind of grape after another. This is a failure; that is better; a third best.
So, bit by bit, they grope about for their Clos
Vougeot and Lafite. Those lodes and pockets of
earth, more precious than the precious ores,
that yield inimitable fragrance and soft fire;
those virtuous Bonanzas, where the soil has
sublimated under sun and stars to something
finer, and the wine is bottled poetry: these still
lie undiscovered; chaparral conceals, thicket
embowers them; the miner chips the rock and
wanders farther, and the grizzly muses undisturbed. But there they bide their hour, awaiting

their Columbus; and nature nurses and prepares them. The smack of Californian earth
shall linger on the palate of your grandson.

Meanwhile the wine is merely a good wine;
the best that I have tasted better than a Beau-
jolais, and not unlike. But the trade is poor; it
lives from hand to mouth, putting its all into
experiments, and forced to sell its vintages. To
find one properly matured, and bearing its own
name, is to be fortune's favourite.

Bearing its own name, I say, and dwell upon the innuendo.

"You want to know why California wine is not
drunk in the States?" a San Francisco wine merchant said to me, after he had shown me through
his premises. "Well, here's the reason."

And opening a large cupboard, fitted with
many little drawers, he proceeded to shower me
all over with a great variety of gorgeously tinted
labels, blue, red, or yellow, stamped with crown
or coronet, and hailing from such a profusion
of *clos* and *châteaux*, that a single department
could scarce have furnished forth the names.

But it was strange that all looked unfamiliar.

"Chateaux X——?" said I. "I never heard of that."

"I dare say not," said he. "I had been reading one of X——'s novels."

They were all castles in Spain! But that sure enough is the reason why California wine is not drunk in the States.

Napa Valley has been long a seat of the wine-growing industry. It did not here begin, as it does too often, in the low valley lands along the river, but took at once to the rough foot-hills, where alone it can expect to prosper. A basking inclination, and stones, to be a reservoir of the day's heat, seem necessary to the soil for wine; the grossness of the earth must be evaporated, its marrow daily melted and refined for ages; until at length these clods that break below our footing, and to the eye appear but common earth, are truly and to the perceiving mind, a masterpiece of nature. The dust of Richebourg, which the wind carries away, what an apotheosis of the dust! Not man himself can seem a stranger child of that brown, friable powder, than the blood and sun in that old flask behind the faggots.

A Californian vineyard, one of man's outposts in the wilderness, has features of its own. There is nothing here to remind you of the Rhine or Rhône, of the low *côte d'or*, or the infamous and scabby deserts of Champagne; but all is green, solitary, covert. We visited two of them, Mr. Schram's and Mr. M'Eckron's, sharing the same glen.

Some way down the valley below Calistoga, we turned sharply to the south and plunged into the thick of the wood. A rude trail rapidly mounting; a little stream tinkling by on the one hand, big enough perhaps after the rains, but already yielding up its life; overhead and on all sides a bower of green and tangled thicket, still fragrant and still flower-bespangled by the early season, where thimble-berry played the part of our English hawthorn, and the buck-eyes were putting forth their twisted horns of blossom: through all this, we struggled toughly up-

wards, canted to and fro by the roughness of
the trail, and continually switched across the
face by sprays of leaf or blossom. The last is no
great inconvenience at home; but here in California it is a matter of some moment. For in all
woods and by every wayside there prospers an
abominable shrub or weed, called poison-oak,
whose very neighbourhood is venomous to some
and whose actual touch is avoided by the most
impervious.

The two houses, with their vineyards, stood
each in a green niche of its own in this steep
and narrow forest dell. Though they were so
near, there was already a good difference in level; and Mr. M'Eckron's head must be a long
way under the feet of Mr. Schram. No more
had been cleared than was necessary for cultivation; close around each oasis ran the tangled
wood; the glen enfolds them; there they lie basking in sun and silence, concealed from all but
the clouds and the mountain birds.

Mr. M'Eckron's is a bachelor establishment;
a little bit of a wooden house, a small cellar hard

by in the hillside, and a patch of vines planted
and tended single-handed by himself. He had
but recently begun; his vines were young, his
business young also; but I thought he had the
look of the man who succeeds. He hailed from
Greenock: he remembered his father putting
him inside Mons Meg, and that touched me
home; and we exchanged a word or two of Scotch
which pleased me more than you would fancy.

Mr. Schram's, on the other hand, is the oldest vineyard in the valley, eighteen years old,
I think; yet he began a penniless barber, and
even after he had broken ground up here with
his black malvoisies, continued for long to tramp
the valley with his razor. Now, his place is the
picture of prosperity: stuffed birds in the verandah, cellars far dug into the hillside, and resting on pillars like a bandit's cave: —all trim-
ness, varnish, flowers, and sunshine, among the
tangled wildwood. Stout, smiling Mrs. Schram,
who has been to Europe and apparently all about
the States for pleasure, entertained Fanny in
the verandah, while I was tasting wines in the

cellar. To Mr. Schram this was a solemn office; his serious gusto warmed my heart; prosperity had not yet wholly banished a certain neophite and girlish trepidation, and he followed every sip and read my face with proud anxiety. I tasted all. I tasted every variety and shade of Schramberger, red and white Schramberger, Burgundy Schramberger, Schramberger Hock, Schramberger Golden Chasselas, the latter with a notable bouquet, and I fear to think how many more. Much of it goes to London — most, I think; and Mr. Schram has a great notion of the English taste.

In this wild spot, I did not feel the sacredness of ancient cultivation. It was still raw, it was no Marathon, and no Johannisberg; yet the stirring sunlight, and the growing vines, and the vats and bottles in the cavern, made a pleasant music for the mind. Here, also, earth's cream was being skimmed and garnered; and the London customers can taste, such as it is, the tang of the earth in this green valley. So local, so quintessential is a wine, that it seems the very birds in the verandah might communicate a flavour, and that romantic cellar influence the bottle next to be uncorked in Pimlico, and the smile of jolly Mr. Schram might mantle in the glass.

But these are but experiments. All things in this new land are moving farther on: the wine-vats and the miner's blasting tools but picket for a night, like Bedouin pavillions; and to-morrow, to fresh woods! This stir of change and these perpetual echoes of the moving footfall, haunt the land. Men move eternally, still chasing Fortune; and, fortune found, still wander. As we drove back to Calistoga, the road lay empty of mere passengers, but its green side was dotted with the camps of travelling families: one cumbered with a great waggonful of household stuff, settlers going to occupy a ranche they had taken up in Mendocino, or perhaps Tehama County; another, a party in dust coats, men and women, whom we found camped in a grove on the roadside, all on pleasure bent, with a China-man to cook for them, and who waved their hands to us as we drove by.

IV.

The Scot Abroad

A few pages back, I wrote that a man belonged, in these days, to a variety of countries; but the old land is still the true love, the others are but pleasant infidelities. Scotland is indefinable; it has no unity except upon the map. Two languages, many dialects, innumerable forms of piety, and countless local patriotisms and prejudices, part us among ourselves more widely than the extreme east and west of that great continent of America. When I am at home, I feel a man from Glasgow to be something like a rival, a man from Barra to be more than half a foreigner. Yet let us meet in some far country,

and, whether we hail from the braes of Manor
or the braes of Mar, some ready-made affection
joins us on the instant. It is not race. Look at us.
One is Norse, one Celtic, and another Saxon.
It is not community of tongue. We have it not
among ourselves; and we have it almost to perfection, with English, or Irish, or American. It
is no tie of faith, for we detest each other's er-
rors. And yet somewhere, deep down in the
heart of each one of us, something yearns for
the old land, and the old kindly people.

Of all mysteries of the human heart, this is
perhaps the most inscrutable. There is no special loveliness in that gray country, with its
rainy, sea-beat archipelago; its fields of dark
mountains; its unsightly places, black with
coal; its treeless, sour, unfriendly looking corn-
lands; its quaint, gray, castled city, where the
bells clash of a Sunday, and the wind squalls,
and the salt showers fly and beat. I do not even
know if I desire to live there; but let me hear,
in some far land, a kindred voice sing out, "Oh,
why left I my hame?" and it seems at once as

if no beauty under the kind heavens, and no society of the wise and good, can repay me for my absence from my country. And though I think I would rather die elsewhere, yet in my heart of hearts I long to be buried among good Scots clods. I will say it fairly, it grows on me with every year: there are no stars so lovely as Edinburgh street-lamps. When I forget thee, auld Reekie, may my right hand forget its cunning!

The happiest lot on earth is to be born a Scotchman. You must pay for it in many ways, as for all other advantages on earth. You have to learn the paraphrases and the shorter catechism; you generally take to drink; your youth, as far as I can find out, is a time of louder war against society, of more outcry and tears and turmoil, than if you had been born, for instance, in England. But somehow life is warmer and closer; the hearth burns more redly; the lights of home shine softer on the rainy street; the very names, endeared in verse and music, cling nearer round our hearts. An Englishman may meet an Englishman to-morrow, upon Chimborazo, and neither of them care; but when the Scotch wine-grower told me of Mons Meg, it was like magic.

"From the dim shieling on the misty island,
Mountains divide us, and a world of seas;
Yet still our hearts are true, our hearts are
Highland,
And we, in dreams, behold the Hebrides."

And, Highland and Lowland, all our hearts are Scotch.

Only a few days after I had seen M'Eckron, a message reached me in my cottage. It was a Scotchman who had come down a long way from the hills to market. He had heard there was a countryman in Calistoga, and came round to the hotel to see him. We said a few words to each other; we had not much to say—should never have seen each other had we stayed at home, separated alike in space and in society; and then we shook hands, and he went his way again to his ranche among the hills, and that was all.

In the Valley

Another Scotchman there was, a resident, who for the mere love of the common country, douce, serious, religious man, drove me all about the valley, and took as much interest in me as if I had been his son: more perhaps; for the son has faults too keenly felt, while the abstract countryman is perfect — like a whiff of peats.

And there was yet another. Upon him I came suddenly, as he was calmly entering my cottage, his mind quite evidently bent on plunder: a man of about fifty, filthy, ragged, roguish, with a chimney-pot hat and a tail coat, and a pursing of his mouth that might have been envied by an elder of the kirk. He had just such a face as I have seen a dozen times behind the plate.

"Hullo, sir!" I cried. "Where are you going?"

He turned round without a quiver.

"You're a Scotchman, sir?" he said gravely. "So am I; I come from Aberdeen. This is my card," presenting me with a piece of pasteboard which he had raked out of some gutter in the period of the rains. "I was just examining this palm," he continued, indicating the misbegotten plant before our door, "which is the largest spæcimen I have yet observed in Califoarnia."

There were four or five larger within sight. But where was the use of argument? He produced a tape-line, made me help him to measure the tree at the level of the ground, and entered the figures in a large and filthy pocketbook, all with the gravity of Solomon. He then thanked me profusely, remarking that such little services were due between countrymen; shook hands with me, "for auld lang syne," as he said; and took himself solemnly away, radiating dirt and humbug as he went.

A month or two after this encounter of mine, there came a Scot to Sacramento—perhaps from Aberdeen. Anyway, there never was any one more Scotch in this wide world. He could sing and dance, and drink, I presume; and he played the pipes with vigour and success. All the Scotch in Sacramento became infatuated with him, and spent their spare time and money, driving him about in an open cab, between drinks, while he blew himself scarlet at the pipes. This is a very sad story. After he had borrowed money from every one, he and his pipes suddenly disappeared from Sacramento, and when I last heard, the police were looking for him.

I cannot say how this story amused me, when I felt myself so thoroughly ripe on both sides to be duped in the same way.

It is at least a curious thing, to conclude, that the races which wander widest, Jews and Scotch, should be the most clannish in the world. But perhaps these two are cause and effect: "For ye were strangers in the land of Egypt."

WITH THE CHILDREN OF ISRAEL

I.

TO INTRODUCE MR. KELMAR

ONE THING in this new country very particularly strikes a stranger, and that is the number of antiquities. Already there have been many cycles of population succeeding each other, and passing away and leaving behind them relics. These, standing on into changed times, strike the imagination as forcibly as any pyramid or feudal tower. The towns, like the vineyards, are experimentally founded: they grow great and prosper by passing occasions; and when the lode comes to an end, and the miners move elsewhere, the town remains behind them, like Palmyra in the desert. I suppose there are, in no country in the world, so many deserted towns as here in California.

The whole neighbourhood of Mount Saint Helena, now so quiet and sylvan, was once alive with mining camps and villages. Here there would be two thousand souls under canvas; there one thousand or fifteen hundred ensconced, as if for ever, in a town of comfortable houses. But the luck had failed, the mines petered out; and the army of miners had departed, and left this quarter of the world to the rattlesnakes and deer and grizzlies, and to the slower but steadier advance of husbandry.

It was with an eye on one of these deserted places, Pine Flat, on the Geysers road, that we had come first to Calistoga. There is something singularly enticing in the idea of going, rent-free, into a ready-made house. And to the British merchant, sitting at home at ease, it may appear that, with such a roof over your head and a spring of clear water hard by, the whole problem of the squatter's existence would be solved. Food, however, has yet to be considered. I will go as far as most people on tinned meats; some of the brightest moments of my life were passed over tinned mulligatawney in the cabin of a sixteen-ton schooner, storm-stayed in Portree Bay; but after suitable experiments, I pronounce authoritatively that man cannot live by tins alone. Fresh meat must be had on an occasion. It is true that the great Foss, driving by along the Geysers road, wooden-faced, but glorified with legend, might have been induced to bring us meat, but the great Foss could hardly bring us milk. To take a cow would have involved taking a field of grass and a milkmaid; after which it would have been hardly worth while to pause, and we might have added to our colony a flock of sheep and an experienced butcher.

It is really very disheartening how we depend on other people in this life. "Mihi est propositum," as you may see by the motto, "id quod regibus;" and behold it cannot be carried out, unless I find a neighbour rolling in cattle.

Now, my principal adviser in this matter was one whom I will call Kelmar. That was not what he called himself, but as soon as I set eyes on him, I knew it was or ought to be his name; I am sure it will be his name among the angels. Kelmar was the store-keeper, a Russian Jew, good-natured, in a very thriving way of business, and, on equal terms, one of the most serviceable of men. He also had something of the expression of a Scotch country elder, who, by some peculiarity, should chance to be a Hebrew. He had a projecting under lip, with which he continually smiled, or rather smirked. Mrs. Kelmar was a singularly kind woman; and the oldest son had quite a dark and romantic bearing, and might be heard on summer evenings playing sentimental airs on the violin.

I had no idea, at the time I made his acquaintance, what an important person Kelmar was. But the Jew storekeepers of California, profiting at once by the needs and habits of the people, have made themselves in too many cases the tyrants of the rural population. Credit is offered, is pressed on the new customer, and when once he is beyond his depth, the tune changes, and he is from thenceforth a white slave. I believe, even from the little I saw, that Kelmar, if he chose to put on the screw, could send half the settlers packing in a radius of seven or eight miles round Calistoga. These are continually paying him but are never suffered to get out of debt. He palms dull goods upon them, for they dare not refuse to buy; he goes and dines with them when he is on an outing, and no man is loudlier welcomed; he is their family friend, the director of their business, and, to a degree elsewhere unknown in modern days, their king.

For some reason, Kelmar always shook his head at the mention of Pine Flat, and for some days I thought he disapproved of the whole scheme and was proportionately sad. One fine morning, however, he met me, wreathed in smiles. He had found the very place for me — Silverado, another old mining town, right up the mountain. Rufe Hanson, the hunter, could take care of us — fine people the Hansons; we should be close to the Toll House, where the

Lakeport stage called daily; it was the best place for my health, besides. Rufe had been consumptive, and was now quite a strong man, ain't it? In short, the place and all its accompaniments seemed made for us on purpose.

He took me to his back door, whence, as from every point of Calistoga, Mount Saint Helena could be seen towering in the air. There, in the nick, just where the eastern foothills joined the mountain, and she herself began to rise above the zone of forest — there was Silverado. The name had already pleased me; the high station pleased me still more. I began to inquire with some eagerness. It was but a little while ago that Silverado was a great place. The mine—a silver mine, of course — had promised great things. There was quite a lively population, with several hotels and boarding-houses; and Kelmar himself had opened a branch store, and done extremely well—"Ain't it?" he said, appealing to his wife. And she said, "Yes; extremely well." Now there was no one living in the town but Rufe the hunter; and once more I heard Rufe's praises by the yard, and this time sung in chorus.

I could not help perceiving at the time that there was something underneath; that no un-mixed desire to have us comfortably settled had inspired the Kelmars with this flow of words. But I was impatient to be gone, to be about my kingly project; and when we were offered seats in Kelmar's waggon, I accepted on the spot. The plan of their next Sunday's outing took them, by good fortune, over the border into Lake County. They would carry us so far, drop us at the Toll House, present us to the Hansons, and call for us again on Monday morning early.

WITH THE CHILDREN
OF ISRAEL
II.
FIRST IMPRESSIONS OF
SILVERADO

WE WERE to leave by six precisely; that was
solemnly pledged on both sides; and a messen-
ger came to us the last thing at night to remind
us of the hour. But it was eight before we got
clear of Calistoga: Kelmar, Mrs. Kelmar, a
friend of theirs whom we named Abramina,
her little daughter, my wife, myself, and, stow-
ed away behind us, a cluster of ship's coffee-
kettles. These last were highly ornamental in
the sheen of their bright tin, but I could invent
no reason for their presence. Our carriageful
reckoned up, as near as we could get at it, some
three hundred years to the six of us. Four of

the six, besides, were Hebrews. But I never, in all my life, was conscious of so strong an atmosphere of holiday. No word was spoken but of pleasure; and even when we drove in silence, nods and smiles went round the party like refreshments.

The sun shone out of a cloudless sky. Close at the zenith rode the belated moon, still clearly visible, and, along one margin, even bright. The wind blew a gale from the north; the trees roared; the corn and the deep grass in the valley fled in whitening surges; the dust towered into the air along the road and dispersed like the smoke of battle. It was clear in our teeth from the first, and for all the windings of the road it managed to keep clear in our teeth until the end.

For some two miles we rattled through the valley, skirting the eastern foothills; then we struck off to the right, through haugh-land, and presently, crossing a dry water-course, entered the Toll road, or, to be more local, entered on "the grade." The road mounts the near shoulder of Mount Saint Helena, bound northward

into Lake County. In one place it skirts along
the edge of a narrow and deep canyon, filled
with trees, and I was glad, indeed, not to be
driven at this point by the dashing Foss. Kelmar, with his unvarying smile, jogging to the
motion of the trap, drove for all the world like
a good, plain, country clergyman at home; and
I profess I blessed him unawares for his timidity.

Vineyards and deep meadows, islanded and
framed with thicket, gave place more and more
as we ascended to woods of oak and madrona,
dotted with enormous pines. It was these pines,
as they shot above the lower wood, that produced that pencilling of single trees I had so
often remarked from the valley. Thence, looking up and from however far, each fir stands
separate against the sky no bigger than an eye-
lash; and all together lend a quaint, fringed as-
pect to the hills. The oak is no baby; even the
madrona, upon these spurs of Mount Saint
Helena, comes to a fine bulk and ranks with
forest trees; but the pines look down upon the
rest for underwood. As Mount Saint Helena

among her foothills, so these dark giants out-
top their fellow-vegetables. Alas! if they had
left the redwoods, the pines, in turn, would
have been dwarfed. But the redwoods, fallen
from their high estate, are serving as family
bedsteads, or yet more humbly as field fences,
along all Napa Valley.

A rough smack of resin was in the air, and
a crystal mountain purity. It came pouring over
these green slopes by the oceanful. The woods
sang aloud, and gave largely of their healthful
breath. Gladness seemed to inhabit these upper
zones, and we had left indifference behind us
in the valley. "I to the hills will lift mine eyes!"
There are days in a life when thus to climb out
of the lowlands, seems like scaling heaven.

As we continued to ascend, the wind fell upon us with increasing strength. It was a wonder
how the two stout horses managed to pull us
up that steep incline and still face the athletic
opposition of the wind, or how their great eyes
were able to endure the dust. Ten minutes after
we went by, a tree fell, blocking the road; and

even before us leaves were thickly strewn, and
boughs had fallen, large enough to make the
passage difficult. But now we were hard by the
summit. The road crosses the ridge, just in the
nick that Kelmar showed me from below, and
then, without pause, plunges down a deep,
thickly wooded glen on the farther side. At the
highest point a trail strikes up the main hill to
the leftward; and that leads to Silverado. A
hundred yards beyond, and in a kind of elbow
of the glen, stands the Toll House Hotel. We
came up the one side, were caught upon the
summit by the whole weight of the wind as it
poured over into Napa Valley, and a minute
after had drawn up in shelter, but all buffeted
and breathless, at the Toll House door.

A water-tank, and stables, and a gray house
of two stories, with gable ends and a verandah,
are jammed hard against the hillside, just where
a stream has cut for itself a narrow canyon, filled
with pines. The pines go right up overhead; a
little more and the stream might have played,
like a fire-hose, on the Toll House roof. In front

the ground drops as sharply as it rises behind. There is just room for the road and a sort of promontory of croquet ground, and then you can lean over the edge and look deep below you through the wood. I said croquet *ground*, not *green;* for the surface was of brown, beaten earth. The toll-bar itself was the only other note of originality: a long beam, turning on a post, and kept slightly horizontal by a counterweight of stones. Regularly about sundown this rude barrier was swung, like a derrick, across the road and made fast, I think, to a tree upon the farther side.

On our arrival there followed a gay scene in the bar. I was presented to Mr. Corwin, the landlord; to Mr. Jennings, the engineer, who lives there for his health; to Mr. Hoddy, a most pleasant little gentleman, once a member of the Ohio legislature, again the editor of a local paper, and now, with undiminished dignity, keeping the Toll House bar. I had a number of drinks and cigars bestowed on me, and enjoyed a famous opportunity of seeing Kelmar in his glo-

ry, friendly, radiant, smiling, steadily edging
one of the ship's kettles on the reluctant Corwin. Corwin, plainly aghast, resisted gallantly,
and for that bout victory crowned his arms.

At last we set forth for Silverado on foot.
Kelmar and his jolly Jew girls were full of the
sentiment of Sunday outings, breathed genial-
ity and vagueness, and suffered a little vile boy
from the hotel to lead them here and there about
the woods. For three people all so old, so bulky
in body, and belonging to a race so venerable,
they could not but surprise us by their extreme
and almost imbecile youthfulness of spirit. They
were only going to stay ten minutes at the Toll
House; had they not twenty long miles of road
before them on the other side? Stay to dinner?
Not they! Put up the horses? Never. Let us at-
tach them to the verandah by a wisp of straw
rope, such as would not have held a person's hat
on that blustering day. And with all these protestations of hurry, they proved irresponsible like
children. Kelmar himself, shrewd old Russian
Jew, with a smirk that seemed just to have con-

cluded a bargain to its satisfaction, intrusted
himself and us devoutly to that boy. Yet the boy
was patently fallacious; and for that matter a
most unsympathetic urchin, raised apparently
on gingerbread. He was bent on his own pleasure, nothing else; and Kelmar followed him to
his ruin, with the same shrewd smirk. If the boy
said there was "a hole there in the hill"—a hole,
pure and simple, neither more nor less—Kelmar
and his Jew girls would follow him a hundred
yards to look complacently down that hole. For
two hours we looked for houses; and for two
hours they followed us, smelling trees, picking
flowers, foisting false botany on the unwary.
Had we taken five, with that vile lad to head
them off on idle divagations, for five they would
have smiled and stumbled through the woods.

However, we came forth at length, and as by
accident, upon a lawn, sparse planted like an
orchard, but with forest instead of fruit trees.
That was the site of Silverado mining town. A
piece of ground was levelled up, where Kelmar's
store had been; and facing that we saw Rufe

Hanson's house, still bearing on its front the legend *Silverado Hotel*. Not another sign of habitation. Silverado town had all been carted from the scene; one of the houses was now the school-house far down the road; one was gone here, one there, but all were gone away. It was now a sylvan solitude, and the silence was unbroken but by the great vague voice of the wind. Some days before our visit, a grizzly bear had been sporting round the Hansons' chicken-house.

Mrs. Hanson was at home alone, we found. Rufe had been out after a "bar," had risen late, and was now gone, it did not clearly appear whither. Perhaps he had had wind of Kelmar's coming, and was now ensconsed among the underwood, or watching us from the shoulder of the mountain. We, hearing there were no houses to be had, were for immediately giving up all hopes of Silverado. But this, somehow, was not to Kelmar's fancy. He first proposed that we should "camp someveres around, ain't it?" waving his hand cheerily as though to weave a spell; and when that was firmly rejected

he decided that we must take up house with
the Hansons. Mrs. Hanson had been, from the
first, flustered, subdued, and a little pale; but
from this proposition she recoiled with haggard
indignation. So did we, who would have pre-
ferred in a manner of speaking, death. But Kelmar was not to be put by. He edged Mrs. Hanson into a corner, where for a long time he threatened her with his forefinger, like a character in
Dickens; and the poor woman, driven to her
entrenchments, at last remembered with a
shriek that there were still some houses at the
tunnel.

Thither we went; the Jews, who should already have been miles into Lake County, still
cheerily accompanying us. For about a furlong
we followed a good road along the hillside
through the forest, until suddenly that road
widened out and came abruptly to an end. A
canyon, woody below, red, rocky, and naked
overhead, was here walled across by a dump
of rolling stones, dangerously steep, and from
twenty to thirty feet in height. A rusty iron

chute on wooden legs came flying, like a monstrous gargoyle, across the parapet. It was down
this that they poured the precious ore; and below here the carts stood to wait their lading,
and carry it mill-ward down the mountain.

The whole canyon was so entirely blocked,
as if by some rude guerilla fortification, that we
could only mount by lengths of wooden ladder,
fixed in the hillside. These led us round the farther corner of the dump; and when they were
at an end, we still persevered over loose rubble
and wading deep in poison-oak, till we struck a
triangular platform, filling up the whole glen,
and shut in on either hand by bold projections
of the mountain. Only in front the place was
open like the proscenium of a theatre, and we
looked forth into a great realm of air, and down
upon treetops and hilltops, and far and near on
wild and varied country. The place still stood
as on the day it was deserted: a line of iron rails
with a bifurcation; a truck in working order;
a world of lumber, old wood, old iron; a blacksmith's forge on one side, half buried in the

leaves of dwarf madronas; and on the other, an old brown wooden house.

Fanny and I dashed at the house. It consisted of three rooms, and was so plastered against the hill, that one room was right atop of another, that the upper floor was more than twice as large as the lower, and that all three apartments must be entered from a different side and level. Not a window-sash remained. The door of the lower room was smashed, and one panel hung in splinters. We entered that, and found a fair amount of rubbish: sand and gravel that had been shifted in there by the mountain winds; straw, sticks, and stones; a table, a barrel; a plate-rack on the wall; two home-made boot-jacks, signs of miners and their boots; and a pair of papers pinned on the boarding, headed respectively "Funnel No. 1," and "Funnel No. 2," but with the tails worn away. The window, sashless of course, was choked with the green and sweetly smelling foliage of a bay; and through a chink in the floor, a spray of poison-oak had shot up and was handsomely prospering in the interior. It was my first care to cut away that poison-oak, Fanny standing by at a respectful distance. That was our first improvement by which we took possession.

The room immediately above could only be entered by a plank propped against the threshold, along which the intruder must foot it gingerly, clutching for support to sprays of poison-oak, the proper product of the country. Herein was, on either hand, a triple tier of beds, where miners had once lain; and the other gable was pierced by a sashless window and a doorless doorway opening on the air of heaven, five feet above the ground. As for the third room, which entered squarely from the ground level, but higher up the hill and further up the canyon, it contained only rubbish and the uprights for another triple tier of beds.

The whole building was overhung by a bold, lion-like, red rock. Poison-oak, sweet bay trees, calcanthus, brush, and chaparral, grew freely but sparsely all about it. In front, in the strong sunshine, the platform lay overstrewn with busy litter, as though the labours of the mine might begin again to-morrow in the morning.

Following back into the canyon, among the mass of rotting plant and through the flowering bushes, we came to a great crazy staging, with a wry windlass on the top; and clambering up, we could look into an open shaft, leading edgeways down into the bowels of the mountain, trickling with water, and lit by some stray sun-gleams, whence I know not. In that quiet place the still, far-away tinkle of the water-drops was loudly audible. Close by, another shaft led edgeways up into the superincumbent shoulder of the hill. It lay partly open; and sixty or a hundred feet above our head, we could see the strata propped apart by solid wooden wedges, and a pine, half undermined, precariously nodding on the verge. Here also a rugged, horizontal tunnel ran straight into the unsunned bowels of the rock. This secure angle in the mountain's flank was, even on this wild day, as still as my lady's chamber. But in the tunnel a cold, wet draught tempestuously blew. Nor have I ever known that place otherwise than cold and windy.

Such was our first prospect of Juan Silverado. I own I had looked for something different: a clique of neighbourly houses on a village green, we shall say, all empty to be sure, but swept and varnished; a trout stream brawling by; great elms or chestnuts, humming with bees and nested in by song birds; and the mountains standing round about, as at Jerusalem. Here, mountain and house and the old tools of industry were all alike rusty and downfalling. The hill was here wedged up, and there poured forth its bowels in a spout of broken mineral; man with his picks and powder, and nature with her own great blasting tools of sun and rain, labouring together at the ruin of that proud mountain. The view up the canyon was a glimpse of devastation; dry red minerals sliding together, here and there a crag, here and there dwarf thicket clinging in the general glissade, and over all a broken outline trenching on the blue of heaven. Downwards indeed, from our rock eyrie, we beheld the greener side of nature; and the bearing of the pines and the sweet smell of bays and nutmegs commended themselves gratefully to our senses. One way and another, now the die was cast. Silverado be it!

After we had got back to the Toll House, the Jews were not long of striking forward. But I observed that one of the Hanson lads came down, before their departure, and returned with a ship's kettle. Happy Hansons! Nor was it until after Kelmar was gone, if I remember rightly, that Rufe put in an appearance to arrange the details of our installation.

The latter part of the day, Fanny and I sat in the verandah of the Toll House, utterly stunned by the uproar of the wind among the trees on the other side of the valley. Sometimes, we would have it it was like a sea, but it was not various enough for that; and again, we thought it like the roar of a cataract, but it was too changeful for the cataract; and then we would decide, speaking in sleepy voices, that it could be compared with nothing but itself. My mind was entirely preoccupied by the noise. I hearkened to it by the hour, gapingly hearkened, and let my cigarette go out. Sometimes the wind would make a sally nearer hand, and send a shrill, whistling crash among the foliage on our side of the glen; and sometimes a back-draught would strike into the elbow where we sat, and cast the gravel and torn leaves into our faces. But for the most part, this great, streaming gale passed unweariedly by us into Napa Valley, not two hundred yards away, visible by the tossing boughs, stunningly audible, and yet not moving a hair upon our heads. So it blew all night long while I was writing up my journal, and after we were in bed, under a cloudless, starset heaven; and so it was blowing still next morning when we rose.

It was a laughable thought to us, what had become of our cheerful, wandering Hebrews. We could not suppose they had reached a destination. The meanest boy could lead them miles out of their way to see a gopher-hole. Boys, we felt to be their special danger; none others were of that exact pitch of cheerful irrelevancy to exercise a kindred sway upon their minds: but before the attractions of a boy their most settled resolutions would be wax. We thought we could follow in fancy these three aged Hebrew truants wandering in and out on hilltop and in thicket, a demon boy trotting far ahead, their will-o'-the-wisp conductor; and at last about midnight, the wind still roaring in the darkness, we had a vision of all three on their knees upon a mountain-top around a glow-worm.

WITH THE CHILDREN
OF ISRAEL

III.

THE RETURN

NEXT MORNING we were up by half-past five,
according to agreement, and it was ten by the
clock before our Jew boys returned to pick us
up: Kelmar, Mrs. Kelmar, and Abramina, all
smiling from ear to ear, and full of tales of the
hospitality they had found on the other side. It
had not gone unrewarded; for I observed with
interest that the ship's kettles, all but one, had
been "placed." Three Lake County families, at
least, endowed for life with a ship's kettle.
Come, this was no misspent Sunday. The absence of the kettles told its own story: our Jews
said nothing about them; but, on the other hand,

they said many kind and comely things about
the people they had met. The two women, in
particular, had been charmed out of themselves
by the sight of a young girl surrounded by her
admirers; all evening, it appeared, they had
been triumphing together in the girl's innocent
successes, and to this natural and unselfish joy
they gave expression in language that was
beautiful by its simplicity and truth.

Take them for all in all, few people have done
my heart more good; they seemed so thoroughly entitled to happiness, and to enjoy it in so
large a measure and so free from after-thought;
almost they persuaded me to be a Jew. There
was, indeed, a chink of money in their talk.
They particularly commended people who were
well to do. "*He* don't care—ain't it?" was their
highest word of commendation to an individual
fate; and here I seem to grasp the root of their
philosophy—it was to be free from care, to be
free to make these Sunday wanderings, that
they so eagerly pursued after wealth; and all
this carefulness was to be careless. The fine,

good humour of all three seemed to declare they
had attained their end. Yet there was the other
side to it; and the recipients of kettles perhaps
cared greatly.

No sooner had they returned, than the scene
of yesterday began again. The horses were not
even tied with a straw rope this time — it was
not worth while; and Kelmar disappeared into
the bar, leaving them under a tree on the other
side of the road. I had to devote myself. I stood
under the shadow of that tree for, I suppose,
hard upon an hour, and had not the heart to be
angry. Once some one remembered me, and
brought me out half a tumblerful of the play-
ful, innocuous American cocktail. I drank it,
and lo! veins of living fire ran down my leg;
and then a focus of conflagration remained
seated in my stomach, not unpleasantly, for
quarter of an hour. I love these sweet, fiery
·pangs, but I will not court them. The bulk of
the time I spent in repeating as much French
poetry as I could remember to the horses, who
seemed to enjoy it hugely. And now it went —

"*O ma vieille Font-georges
Où volent les rouges-gorges:*"

and again, to a more trampling measure —

"*Et tout tremble, Irun, Coïmbre,
Santander, Almodovar,
Sitôt qu'on entend le timbre
Des cymbales de Bivar.*"

The redbreasts and the brooks of Europe, in that dry and songless land; brave old names and wars, strong cities, cymbals, and bright armour, in that nook of the mountain, sacred only to the Indian and the bear! This is still the strangest thing in all man's travelling, that he should carry about with him incongruous memories. There is no foreign land; it is the traveller only that is foreign, and now and again, by a flash of recollection, lights up the contrasts of the earth.

But while I was thus wandering in my fancy, great feats had been transacted in the bar. Corwin the bold had fallen, Kelmar was again

crowned with laurels, and the last of the ship's
kettles had changed hands. If I had ever doubted
the purity of Kelmar's motives, if I had ever
suspected him of a single eye to business in his
eternal dallyings, now at least, when the last
kettle was disposed of, my suspicions must have
been allayed. I dare not guess how much more
time was wasted; nor how often we drove off,
merely to drive back again and renew interrupted conversations about nothing, before the
Toll House was fairly left behind. Alas! and
not a mile down the grade there stands a ranche
in a sunny vineyard, and here we must all dis-
mount again and enter.

Only the old lady was at home, Mrs. Guele,
a brown old Swiss dame, the picture of honesty;
and with her we drank a bottle of wine and had
an age-long conversation, which would have
been highly delightful if Fanny and I had not
been faint with hunger. The ladies each nar-
rated the story of her marriage, our two Hebrews with the prettiest combination of sentiment and financial bathos. Abramina, specially,

endeared herself with every word. She was as simple, natural, and engaging as a kid that should have been brought up to the business of a money-changer. One touch was so resplendently Hebraic that I cannot pass it over. When her "old man" wrote home for her from America, her old man's family would not intrust her with the money for the passage, till she had bound herself by an oath—on her knees, I think she said—not to employ it otherwise. This had tickled Abramina hugely, but I think it tickled me fully more.

Mrs. Guele told of her home-sickness up here in the long winters; of her honest, country-woman troubles and alarms upon the journey; how in the bank at Frankfort she had feared lest the banker, after having taken her cheque, should deny all knowledge of it—a fear I have myself every time I go to a bank; and how crossing the Luneburger Heath, an old lady, witnessing her trouble and finding whither she was bound, had given her "the blessing of a person eighty years old, which would be sure

to bring her safely to the States. And the first
thing I did,'' added Mrs. Guele, "was to fall
downstairs.''

At length we got out of the house, and some
of us into the trap, when—judgment of Heav-
en!—here came Mr. Guele from his vineyard.
So another quarter of an hour went by; till at
length, at our earnest pleading, we set forth
again in earnest, Fanny and I white-faced and
silent, but the Jews still smiling. The heart fails
me. There was yet another stoppage! And we
drove at last into Calistoga past two in the afternoon, Fanny and I having breakfasted at six
in the morning, eight mortal hours before. We
were a pallid couple; but still the Jews were
smiling.

So ended our excursion with the village usur-
ers; and, now that it was done, we had no more
idea of the nature of the business, nor of the
part we had been playing in it, than the child
unborn. That all the people we had met were
the slaves of Kelmar, though in various degrees
of servitude; that we ourselves had been sent

up the mountain in the interests of none but
Kelmar; that the money we laid out, dollar by
dollar, cent by cent, and through the hands of
various intermediaries, should all hop ultimate-
ly into Kelmar's till;—these were facts that we
only grew to recognize in the course of time and
by the accumulation of evidence. At length all
doubt was quieted, when one of the kettle-
holders confessed. Stopping his trap in the
moonlight, a little way out of Calistoga, he told
me in so many words, that he dare not show face
there with an empty pocket. "You see, I don't
mind if it was only five dollars, Mr. Stevens,"
he said, "but I must give Mr. Kelmar *something*."

Even now, when the whole tyranny is plain
to me, I cannot find it in my heart to be as angry as perhaps I should be with the Hebrew
tyrant. The whole game of business is beggar
my neighbour; and though perhaps that game
looks uglier when played at such close quarters
and on so small a scale, it is none the more intrin-
sically inhumane for that. The village usurer is

not so sad a feature of humanity and human progress as the millionaire manufacturer, fattening on the toil and loss of thousands, and yet declaiming from the platform against the greed and dishonesty of landlords. If it were fair for Cobden to buy up land from owners whom he thought unconscious of its proper value, it was fair enough for my Russian Jew to give credit to his farmers. Kelmar, if he was unconscious of the beam in his own eye, was at least silent in the matter of his brother's mote.

THE
ACT OF SQUATTING

THERE WERE four of us squatters — myself and my wife, the King and Queen of Silverado; Sam, the Crown Prince; and Chuchu, the Grand Duke. Chuchu, a setter crossed with spaniel, was the most unsuited for a rough life. He had been nurtured tenderly in the society of ladies; his heart was large and soft; he regarded the sofa-cushion as a bed-rock necessary of existence. Though about the size of a sheep, he loved to sit in ladies' laps; he never said a bad word in all his blameless days; and if he had seen a flute, I am sure he could have played upon it by nature. It may seem hard to say it of a dog, but Chuchu was a tame cat.

The king and queen, the grand duke, and a basket of cold provender for immediate use, set forth from Calistoga in a double buggy; the crown prince, on horseback, led the way like an outrider. Bags and boxes and a second-hand stove were to follow close upon our heels by Hanson's team.

It was a beautiful still day; the sky was one field of azure. Not a leaf moved, not a speck appeared in heaven. Only from the summit of the mountain one little snowy wisp of cloud after another kept detaching itself, like smoke from a volcano, and blowing southward in some high stream of air: Mount Saint Helena still at her interminable task, making the weather, like a Lapland witch.

By noon we had come in sight of the mill: a great brown building, half-way up the hill, big as a factory, two stories high, and with tanks and ladders along the roof; which, as a pendicle of Silverado mine, we held to be an outlying province of our own. Thither, then, we went, crossing the valley by a grassy trail; and there lunched out of the basket, sitting in a kind of portico, and wondering, while we ate, at this great bulk of useless building. Through a chink we could look far down into the interior, and see sunbeams floating in the dust and striking on tier after tier of silent, rusty machinery. It cost six thousand dollars, twelve hundred English sovereigns; and now, here it stands deserted, like the temple of a forgotten religion, the busy millers toiling somewhere else. All the time we were there, mill and mill town showed no sign of life; that part of the mountain-side, which is very open and green, was tenanted by no living creature but ourselves and the insects; and nothing stirred but the cloud manufactory upon the mountain summit. It was odd to compare this with the former days, when the engine was in full blast, the mill palpitating to its strokes, and the carts came rattling down from Silverado, charged with ore.

By two we had been landed at the mine, the

buggy was gone again, and we were left to our own reflections and the basket of cold provender, until Hanson should arrive. Hot as it was by the sun, there was something chill in such a home-coming, in that world of wreck and rust, splinter and rolling gravel, where for so many years no fire had smoked.

Silverado platform filled the whole width of the canyon. Above, as I have said, this was a wild, red, stony gully in the mountains; but below it was a wooded dingle. And through this, I was told, there had gone a path between the mine and the Toll House—our natural northwest passage to civilization. I found and followed it, clearing my way as I went through fallen branches and dead trees. It went straight down that steep canyon, till it brought you out abruptly over the roofs of the hotel. There was nowhere any break in the descent. It almost seemed as if, were you to drop a stone down the old iron chute at our platform, it would never rest until it hopped upon the Toll House shingles. Signs were not wanting of the ancient greatness of Silverado. The footpath was well marked, and had been well trodden in the old days by thirsty miners. And far down, buried in foliage, deep out of sight of Silverado, I came on a last outpost of the mine—a mound of gravel, some wreck of wooden aqueduct, and the mouth of a tunnel, like a treasure grotto in a fairy story. A stream of water, fed by the invisible leakage from our shaft, and dyed red with cinnabar or iron, ran trippingly forth out of the bowels of the cave; and, looking far under the arch, I could see something like an iron lantern fastened on the rocky wall. It was a promising spot for the imagination. No boy could have left it unexplored.

The stream thenceforward stole along the bottom of the dingle, and made, for that dry land, a pleasant warbling in the leaves. Once, I suppose, it ran splashing down the whole length of the canyon, but now its head waters had been tapped by the shaft at Silverado, and for a great part of its course it wandered sunless among the joints of the mountain. No wonder

that it should better its pace when it sees, far
before it, daylight whitening in the arch, or that
it should come trotting forth into the sunlight
with a song.

The two stages had gone by when I got
down, and the Toll House stood, dozing in sun
and dust and silence, like a place enchanted.
My mission was after hay for bedding, and that
I was readily promised. But when I mentioned
that we were waiting for Rufe, the people shook
their heads. Rufe was not a regular man any
way, it seemed; and if he got playing poker —
Well, poker was too many for Rufe. I had not
yet heard them bracketted together; but it
seemed a natural conjunction, and commended
itself swiftly to my fears; and as soon as I returned to Silverado and had told my story, we
practically gave Hanson up, and set ourselves
to do what we could find do-able in our desert-
island state.

The lower room had been the assayer's office.
The floor was thick with *débris* — part human,
from the former occupants; part natural, sifted

in by mountain winds. In a sea of red dust there swam or floated sticks, boards, hay, straw, stones, and paper; ancient newspapers, above all—for the newspaper, especially when torn, soon becomes an antiquity—and bills of the Silverado boarding-house, some dated Silverado, some Calistoga Mine. Here is one, verbatim; and if anyone can calculate the scale of charges, he has my envious admiration.

Calistoga Mine, May 3rd, 1875.

John Stanley
  To S. Chapman, Cʳ.

To board from April 1st, to April 30th		$25	75
" " " May 1st, to 3rd		2	00
		27	75

Where is John Stanley mining now? Where is S. Chapman, within whose hospitable walls we were to lodge? The date was but five years old, but in that time the world had changed for Silverado; like Palmyra in the desert, it had outlived its people and its purpose; we camped, like Layard, amid ruins, and these names spoke to us of pre-historic time. A boot-jack, a pair of boots, a dog-hutch, and these bills of Mr. Chapman's were the only speaking relics that we disinterred from all that vast Silverado rubbish-heap; but what would I not have given to unearth a letter, a pocket-book, a diary, only a ledger, or a roll of names, to take me back, in a more personal manner, to the past? It pleases me, besides, to fancy that Stanley or Chapman, or one of their companions, may light upon this chronicle, and be struck by the name, and read some news of their anterior home, coming, as it were, out of a subsequent epoch of history in that quarter of the world.

As we were tumbling the mingled rubbish on the floor, kicking it with our feet, and groping for these written evidences of the past, Sam, with a somewhat whitened face, produced a paper bag. "What's this?" said he. It contained a granulated powder, something the colour of Gregory's Mixture, but rosier; and as there were several of the bags, and each more or less broken, the powder was spread widely on the floor. Had any of us ever seen giant powder?

No, nobody had; and instantly there grew up in my mind a shadowy belief, verging with every moment nearer to certitude, that I had somewhere heard somebody describe it as just such a powder as the one around us. I have learnt since that it is a substance not unlike tallow, and is made up in rolls for all the world like tallow candles.

Fanny, to add to our happiness, told us a story of a gentleman who had camped one night, like ourselves, by a deserted mine. He was a handy, thrifty fellow, and looked right and left for plunder, but all he could lay his hands on was a can of oil. After dark he had to see to the horses with a lantern; and not to miss an opportunity, filled up his lamp from the oil can. Thus equipped, he set forth into the forest. A little while after, his friends heard a loud explosion; the mountain echoes bellowed, and then all was still. On examination, the can proved to contain oil, with the trifling addition of nitro-glycerine; but no research disclosed a trace of either man or lantern.

The Act of Squatting

It was a pretty sight, after this anecdote, to see us sweeping out the giant powder. It seemed never to be far enough away. And, after all, it was only some rock pounded for assay.

So much for the lower room. We scraped some of the rougher dirt off the floor, and left it. That was our sitting-room and kitchen, though there was nothing to sit upon but the table, and no provision for a fire except a hole in the roof of the room above, which had once contained the chimney of a stove.

To that upper room we now proceeded. There were the eighteen bunks in a double tier, nine on either hand, where from eighteen to thirty-six miners had once snored together all night long, John Stanley, perhaps, snoring loudest. There was the roof, with a hole in it through which the sun now shot an arrow. There was the floor, in much the same state as the one below, though, perhaps, there was more hay, and certainly there was the added ingredient of broken glass, the man who stole the window-frames having apparently made a miscarriage

with this one. Without a broom, without hay
or bedding, we could but look about us with a
beginning of despair. The one bright arrow of
day, in that gaunt and shattered barrack, made
the rest look dirtier and darker, and the sight
drove us at last into the open.

Here, also, the handiwork of man lay ruined:
but the plants were all alive and thriving; the
view below was fresh with the colours of nature; and we had exchanged a dim, human
garret for a corner, even although it were un-
tidy, of the blue hall of heaven. Not a bird, not
a beast, not a reptile. There was no noise in that
part of the world, save when we passed beside
the staging, and heard the water musically falling in the shaft.

We wandered to and fro. We searched among
that drift of lumber —wood and iron, nails and
rails, and sleepers and the wheels of trucks.
We gazed up the cleft into the bosom of the
mountain. We sat by the margin of the dump
and saw, far below us, the green treetops standing still in the clear air. Beautiful perfumes,

breaths of bay, resin, and nutmeg, came to us
more often and grew sweeter and sharper as
the afternoon declined. But still there was no
word of Hanson.

I set to with pick and shovel, and deepened
the pool behind the shaft, till we were sure of
sufficient water for the morning; and by the
time I had finished, the sun had begun to go
down behind the mountain shoulder, the platform was plunged in quiet shadow, and a chill
descended from the sky. Night began early in
our cleft. Before us, over the margin of the
dump, we could see the sun still striking aslant
into the wooded nick below, and on the battle-
mented, pine-bescattered ridges on the farther
side.

There was no stove, of course, and no hearth
in our lodging, so we betook ourselves to the
blacksmith's forge across the platform. If the
platform be taken as a stage, and the out-curv-
ing margin of the dump to represent the line of
the footlights, then our house would be the first
wing on the actor's left, and this blacksmith's

forge, although no match for it in size, the foremost on the right. It was a low, brown cottage, planted close against the hill, and overhung by the foliage and peeling boughs of a madrona thicket. Within it was full of dead leaves and mountain dust, and rubbish from the mine. But we soon had a good fire brightly blazing, and sat close about it on impromptu seats. Chuchu, the slave of sofa-cushions, whimpered for a softer bed; but the rest of us were greatly revived and comforted by that good creature — fire, which gives us warmth and light and companionable sounds, and colours up the emptiest building with better than frescoes. For a while it was even pleasant in the forge, with the blaze in the midst, and a look over our shoulders on the woods and mountains where the day was dying like a dolphin.

It was between seven and eight before Hanson arrived, with a waggonful of our effects and two of his wife's relatives to lend him a hand. The elder showed surprising strength. He would pick up a huge packing-case, full of books of

all things, swing it on his shoulder, and away
up the two crazy ladders and the breakneck
spout of rolling mineral, familiarly termed a
path, that led from the cart-track to our house.
Even for a man unburthened, the ascent was
toilsome and precarious; but Irvine scaled it
with a light foot, carrying box after box, as the
hero whisks the stage child up the practicable
footway beside the waterfall of the fifth act.
With so strong a helper, the business was speed-
ily transacted. Soon the assayer's office was
thronged with our belongings, piled higgledy-
piggledy, and upside down, about the floor.
There were our boxes, indeed, but my wife had
left her keys in Calistoga. There was the stove,
but, alas! our carriers had forgot the chimney,
and lost one of the plates along the road. The
Silverado problem was scarce solved.

Rufe himself was grave and good-natured
over his share of blame; he even, if I remember
right, expressed regret. But his crew, to my as-
tonishment and anger, grinned from ear to ear,
and laughed aloud at our distress. They thought

it "real funny" about the stove-pipe they had
forgotten; "real funny" that they should have
lost a plate. As for hay, the whole party refused to bring us any till they should have
supped. See how late they were! Never had
there been such a job as coming up that grade!
Nor often, I suspect, such a game of poker as
that before they started. But about nine, as a
particular favour, we should have some hay.

So they took their departure, leaving me still
staring, and we resigned ourselves to wait for
their return. The fire in the forge had been suffered to go out, and we were one and all too
weary to kindle another. We dined, or, not to
take that word in vain, we ate after a fashion,
in the nightmare disorder of the assayer's office,
perched among boxes. A single candle lighted
us. It could scarce be called a house-warming;
for there was, of course, no fire, and with the
two open doors and the open window gaping
on the night, like breaches in a fortress, it began to grow rapidly chill. Talk ceased; nobody
moved but the unhappy Chuchu, still in quest

of sofa-cushions, who tumbled complainingly among the trunks. It required a certain happiness of disposition to look forward hopefully, from so dismal a beginning, across the brief hours of night, to the warm shining of to-morrow's sun.

But the hay arrived at last, and we turned, with our last spark of courage, to the bedroom. We had improved the entrance, but it was still a kind of rope-walking; and it would have been droll to see us mounting, one after another, by candle-light under the open stars.

The western door — that which looked up the canyon, and through which we entered by our bridge of flying plank — was still entire, a handsome, panelled door, the most finished piece of carpentry in Silverado. And the two lowest bunks next to this we roughly filled with hay for that night's use. Through the opposite, or eastern-looking gable, with its open door and window, a faint, diffused starshine came into the room like mist; and when we were once in bed, we lay awaiting sleep, in a haunted, incomplete obscurity. At first the silence of the night was utter. Then a high wind began in the distance among the treetops, and for hours continued to grow higher. It seemed to me much such a wind as we had found on our visit; yet here in our open chamber we were fanned only by gentle and refreshing draughts, so deep was the canyon, so close our house was planted under the overhanging rock.

THE HUNTER'S FAMILY

THERE IS quite a large race or class of people in America, for whom we scarcely seem to have a parallel in England. Of pure white blood, they are unknown or unrecognizable in towns; inhabit the fringe of settlements and the deep, quiet places of the country; rebellious to all labour, and pettily thievish, like the English gipsies; rustically ignorant, but with a touch of wood-lore and the dexterity of the savage. Whence they came is a moot point. At the time of the war, they poured north in crowds to escape the conscription; lived during summer on fruits, wild animals, and petty theft; and at the

approach of winter, when these supplies failed,
built great fires in the forest, and there died sto-
ically by starvation. They are widely scattered,
however, and easily recognized. Loutish, but
not ill-looking, they will sit all day, swinging
their legs on a field fence, the mind seemingly
as devoid of all reflection as a Suffolk peasant's,
careless of politics, for the most part incapable
of reading, but with a rebellious vanity and a
strong sense of independence. Hunting is their
most congenial business, or, if the occasion
offers, a little amateur detection. In tracking a
criminal, following a particular horse along a
beaten highway, and drawing inductions from
a hair or a footprint, one of those somnolent,
grinning Hodges will suddenly display activity
of body and finesse of mind. By their names ye
may know them, the women figuring as Love-
ina, Larsenia, Serena, Leanna, Orreana; the
men answering to Alvin, Alva, or Orion, pro-
nounced Orrion, with the accent on the first.
Whether they are indeed a race, or whether this
is the form of degeneracy common to all back-

woodsmen, they are at least known by a generic byword, as Poor Whites or Low-downers.

I will not say that the Hanson family was Poor White, because the name savours of offence; but I may go as far as this — they were, in many points, not unsimilar to the people usually so-called. Rufe himself combined two of the qualifications, for he was both a hunter and an amateur detective. It was he who pursued Russel and Dollar, the robbers of the Lakeport stage, and captured them the very morning after the exploit, while they were still sleeping in a hayfield. Russel, a drunken Scotch carpenter, was even an acquaintance of his own, and he expressed much grave commiseration for his fate. In all that he said and did, Rufe was grave. I never saw him hurried. When he spoke, he took out his pipe with ceremonial deliberation, looked east and west, and then, in quiet tones and few words, stated his business or told his story. His gait was to match; it would never have surprised you if, at any step, he had turned round and walked away again, so warily and

slowly, and with so much seeming hesitation
did he go about. He lay long in bed in the morning—rarely indeed, rose before noon; he loved
all games, from poker to clerical croquet; and
in the Toll House croquet ground I have seen
him toiling at the latter with the devotion of a
curate. He took an interest in education, was an
active member of the local school-board, and
when I was there, he had recently lost the school-
house key. His waggon was broken, but it never seemed to occur to him to mend it. Like all
truly idle people, he had an artistic eye. He chose
the print stuff for his wife's dresses, and coun-
selled her in the making of a patchwork quilt,
always, as she thought, wrongly, but to the more
educated eye, always with bizarre and admirable
taste—the taste of an Indian. With all this, he
was a perfect, unoffending gentleman in word
and act. Take his clay pipe from him, and he was
fit for any society but that of fools. Quiet as he
was, there burned a deep, permanent excitement
in his dark blue eyes; and when this grave man
smiled, it was like sunshine in a shady place.

The Hunter's Family

Mrs. Hanson (*née*, if you please, Lovelands) was more commonplace than her lord. She was a comely woman, too, plump, fair-coloured, with wonderful white teeth; and in her print dresses (chosen by Rufe) and with a large sunbonnet shading her valued complexion, made, I assure you, a very agreeable figure. But she was on the surface, what there was of her, outspoken and loud-spoken. Her noisy laughter had none of the charm of one of Hanson's rare, slow-spreading smiles; there was no reticence, no mystery, no manner about the woman: she was a first-class dairymaid, but her husband was an unknown quantity between the savage and the nobleman. She was often in and out with us, merry, and healthy, and fair; he came far seldomer—only, indeed, when there was business, or now and again, to pay a visit of ceremony, brushed up for the occasion, with his wife on his arm, and a clean clay pipe in his teeth. These visits, in our forest state, had quite the air of an event, and turned our red canyon into a salon.

Such was the pair who ruled in the old Silverado Hotel, among the windy trees, on the mountain shoulder overlooking the whole length of Napa Valley, as the man aloft looks down on the ship's deck. There they kept house, with sundry horses and fowls, and a family of sons, Daniel Webster, and I think George Washington, among the number. Nor did they want visitors. An old gentleman, of singular stolidity, and called Breedlove — I think he had crossed the plains in the same caravan with Rufe — housed with them for awhile during our stay; and they had besides a permanent lodger, in the form of Mrs. Hanson's brother, Irvine Lovelands. I spell Irvine by guess; for I could get no information on the subject, just as I could never find out, in spite of many inquiries, whether or not Rufe was a contraction for Rufus. They were all cheerfully at sea about their names in that generation. And this is surely the more notable where the names are all so strange, and even the family names appear to have been coined. At one time, at least, the ancestors of all these Alvins and Alvas, Loveinas, Lovelands, and Breedloves, must have taken serious council and found a certain poetry in these denominations; that must have been, then, their form of literature. But still times change; and their next descendants, the George Washingtons and Daniel Websters, will at least be clear upon the point. And anyway, and however his name should be spelt, this Irvine Lovelands was the most unmitigated Caliban I ever knew.

Our very first morning at Silverado, when we were full of business, patching up doors and windows, making beds and seats, and getting our rough lodging into shape, Irvine and his sister made their appearance together, she for neighbourliness and general curiosity; he, because he was working for me, to my sorrow, cutting firewood at I forget how much a day. The way that he set about cutting wood was characteristic. We were at that moment patching up and unpacking in the kitchen. Down he sat on one side, and down sat his sister on the other. Both were chewing pine-tree gum, and he, to my annoyance, accompanied that simple pleasure with profuse expectoration. She rattled away, talking up hill and down dale, laughing, tossing her head, showing her brilliant teeth. He looked on in silence, now spitting heavily on the floor, now putting his head back and uttering a loud, discordant, joyless laugh. He had a tangle of shock hair, the colour of wool; his mouth was a grin; although as strong as a horse, he looked neither heavy nor yet adroit, only leggy, coltish, and in the road. But it was plain he was in high spirits, thoroughly enjoying his visit; and he laughed frankly whenever we failed to accomplish what we were about. This was scarcely helpful: it was even, to amateur carpenters, embarrassing; but it lasted until we knocked off work and began to get dinner. Then Mrs. Hanson remembered she should have been gone an hour ago; and the pair retired, and the lady's laughter died away among the nutmegs down the path. That was Irvine's first day's work in my employment — the devil take him!

The next morning he returned and, as he was

this time alone, he bestowed his conversation upon us with great liberality. He prided himself on his intelligence; asked us if we knew the school ma'am. *He* didn't think much of her, anyway. He had tried her, he had. He had put a question to her. If a tree a hundred feet high were to fall a foot a day, how long would it take to fall right down? She had not been able to solve the problem. "She don't know nothing," he opined. He told us how a friend of his kept a school with a revolver, and chuckled mightily over that; his friend could teach school, he could. All the time he kept chewing gum and spitting. He would stand a while looking down; and then he would toss back his shock of hair, and laugh hoarsely, and spit, and bring forward a new subject. A man, he told us, who bore a grudge against him, had poisoned his dog. "That was a low thing for a man to do now, wasn't it? It wasn't like a man, that, nohow. But I got even with him: I pisoned *his* dog." This clumsy utterance, his rude embarrassed manner, set a fresh value on the stupidity of

his remarks. I do not think I ever appreciated
the meaning of two words until I knew Irvine—
the verb, loaf, and the noun, oaf; between them,
they complete his portrait. He could lounge,
and wriggle, and rub himself against the wall,
and grin, and be more in everybody's way than
any other two people that I ever set my eyes on.
Nothing that he did became him; and yet you
were conscious that he was one of your own
race, that his mind was cumbrously at work,
revolving the problem of existence like a quid
of gum, and in his own cloudy manner enjoying life, and passing judgment on his fellows.
Above all things, he was delighted with himself. You would not have thought it, from his
uneasy manners and troubled, struggling utterance; but he loved himself to the marrow, and
was happy and proud like a peacock on a rail.

His self-esteem was, indeed, the one joint in
his harness. He could be got to work, and even
kept at work, by flattery. As long as my wife
stood over him, crying out how strong he was,
so long exactly he would stick to the matter

in hand; and the moment she turned her back,
or ceased to praise him, he would stop. His
physical strength was wonderful; and to have
a woman stand by and admire his achieve-
ments, warmed his heart like sunshine. Yet
he was as cowardly as he was powerful, and
felt no shame in owning to the weakness.
Something was once wanted from the crazy
platform over the shaft, and he at once refused
to venture there — "did not like," as he said,
"foolen' round them kind o' places," and let
my wife go instead of him, looking on with a
grin. Vanity, where it rules, is usually more
heroic: but Irvine steadily approved himself,
and expected others to approve him; rather
looked down upon my wife, and decidedly expected her to look up to him, on the strength of
his superior prudence.

Yet the strangest part of the whole matter
was perhaps this, that Irvine was as beautiful
as a statue. His features were, in themselves,
perfect; it was only his cloudy, uncouth, and
coarse expression that disfigured them. So

much strength residing in so spare a frame was proof sufficient of the accuracy of his shape. He must have been built somewhat after the pattern of Jack Sheppard; but the famous housebreaker, we may be certain, was no lout. It was by the extraordinary powers of his mind no less than by the vigour of his body, that he broke his strong prison with such imperfect implements, turning the very obstacles to service. Irvine, in the same case, would have sat down and spat, and grumbled curses. He had the soul of a fat sheep, but, regarded as an artist's model, the exterior of a Greek God. It was a cruel thought to persons less favoured in their birth, that this creature, endowed—to use the language of theatres—with extraordinary "means," should so manage to misemploy them that he looked ugly and almost deformed. It was only by an effort of abstraction, and after many days, that you discovered what he was.

By playing on the oaf's conceit, and standing closely over him, we got a path made round the corner of the dump to our door, so that we

could come and go with decent ease; and he
even enjoyed the work, for in that there were
boulders to be plucked up bodily, bushes to be
uprooted, and other occasions for athletic display: but cutting wood was a different matter.
Anybody could cut wood; and, besides, my wife
was tired of supervising him, and had other
things to attend to. And, in short, days went
by, and Irvine came daily, and talked and
lounged and spat; but the firewood remained
intact as sleepers on the platform or growing
trees upon the mountain-side. Irvine, as a wood-
cutter, we could tolerate; but Irvine as a friend
of the family, at so much a day, was too bald
an imposition, and at length, on the afternoon
of the fourth or fifth day of our connection, I
explained to him, as clearly as I could, the light
in which I had grown to regard his presence.
I pointed out to him that I could not continue
to give him a salary for spitting on the floor;
and this expression, which came after a good
many others, at last penetrated his obdurate
wits. He rose at once, and said that if that was

the way he was going to be spoke to, he reckoned he would quit. And, no one interposing, he departed.

So far, so good. But we had no firewood. The next afternoon, I strolled down to Rufe's and consulted him on the subject. It was a very droll interview, in the large, bare north room of the Silverado Hotel, Mrs. Hanson's patchwork on a frame, and Rufe, and his wife, and I, and the oaf himself, all more or less embarrassed. Rufe announced there was nobody in the neighbourhood but Irvine who could do a day's work for anybody. Irvine, thereupon, refused to have any more to do with my service; he "wouldn't work no more for a man as had spoke to him's I had done." I found myself on the point of the last humiliation—driven to beseech the creature whom I had just dismissed with insult: but I took the high hand in despair, said there must be no talk of Irvine coming back unless matters were to be differently managed; that I would rather chop firewood for myself than be fooled; and, in short, the Hansons being eager for the lad's hire, I so imposed upon them with merely affected resolution, that they ended by begging me to re-employ him again, on a solemn promise that he should be more industrious. The promise, I am bound to say, was kept. We soon had a fine pile of firewood at our door; and if Caliban gave me the cold shoulder and spared me his conversation, I thought none the worse of him for that, nor did I find my days much longer for the deprivation.

The leading spirit of the family was, I am inclined to fancy, Mrs. Hanson. Her social brilliancy somewhat dazzled the others, and she had more of the small change of sense. It was she who faced Kelmar, for instance; and perhaps, if she had been alone, Kelmar would have had no rule within her doors. Rufe, to be sure, had a fine, sober, open-air attitude of mind, seeing the world without exaggeration—perhaps, we may even say, without enough; for he lacked along with the others, that commercial idealism which puts so high a value on time and money. Sanity itself is a kind of convention. Perhaps

Rufe was wrong; but, looking on life plainly, he was unable to perceive that croquet or poker were in any way less important than, for instance, mending his waggon. Even his own profession, hunting, was dear to him mainly as a sort of play; even that he would have neglected had it not appealed to his imagination. His hunting-suit, for instance, had cost I should be afraid to say how many bucks — the currency in which he paid his way: it was all befringed after the Indian fashion, and it was dear to his heart. The pictorial side of his daily business was never forgotten. He was even anxious to stand for his picture in those buckskin hunting clothes; and I remember how he once warmed almost into enthusiasm, his dark blue eyes growing perceptibly larger, as he planned the composition in which he should appear, "with the horns of some real big bucks, and dogs, and a camp on a crick" (creek, stream).

There was no trace in Irvine of this woodland poetry. He did not care for hunting, nor yet for buckskin suits. He had never observed scenery.

The world, as it appeared to him, was almost obliterated by his own great grinning figure in the foreground: Caliban Malvolio. And it seems to me as if, in the persons of these brothers-in-law, we had the two sides of rusticity fairly well represented: the hunter living really in nature; the clodhopper living merely out of society: the one bent up in every corporal agent to capacity in one pursuit, doing at least one thing keenly and thoughtfully, and thoroughly alive to all that touches it; the other in the inert and bestial state, walking in a faint dream, and taking so dim an impression of the myriad sides of life that he is truly conscious of nothing but himself. It is only in the fastnesses of nature, forests, mountains, and the back of man's beyond, that a creature endowed with five senses can grow up into the perfection of this crass and earthy vanity. In towns or the busier country sides, he is roughly reminded of other men's existence; and if he learns no more, he learns at least to fear contempt. But Irvine had come scatheless through life, conscious only of himself, of his great strength and intelligence; and in the silence of the universe, to which he did not listen, dwelling with delight on the sound of his own thoughts.

The Sea Fogs

A CHANGE in the colour of the light usually called me in the morning. By a certain hour, the long, vertical chinks in our western gable, where the boards had shrunk and separated, flashed suddenly into my eyes as stripes of dazzling blue, at once so dark and splendid that I used to marvel how the qualities could be combined. At an earlier hour, the heavens in that quarter were still quietly coloured, but the shoulder of the mountain which shuts in the canyon already glowed with sunlight in a wonderful compound of gold and rose and green; and this too would kindle, although more mildly and with rainbow tints, the fissures of our crazy gable. If I were sleeping heavily, it was the bold blue that struck me awake; if more lightly, then I would come to myself in that earlier and fairier light.

One Sunday morning, about five, the first brightness called me. I rose and turned to the east, not for my devotions, but for air. The night had been very still. The little private gale that blew every evening in our canyon, for ten minutes or perhaps a quarter of an hour, had swiftly blown itself out; in the hours that followed not a sigh of wind had shaken the treetops; and our barrack, for all its breaches, was less fresh that morning than of wont. But I had no sooner reached the window than I forgot all else in the sight that met my eyes, and I made but two bounds into my clothes, and down the crazy plank to the platform.

The sun was still concealed below the opposite hilltops, though it was shining already, not twenty feet above my head, on our mountain slope. But the scene, beyond a few near features,

was entirely changed. Napa Valley was gone;
gone were all the lower slopes and woody foot-
hills of the range; and in their place, not a thousand feet below me, rolled a great level ocean.
It was as though I had gone to bed the night
before, safe in a nook of inland mountains, and
had awakened in a bay upon the coast. I had
seen these inundations from below; at Calistoga
I had risen and gone abroad in the early morning, coughing and sneezing, under fathoms on
fathoms of gray sea vapour, like a cloudy sky —
a dull sight for the artist, and a painful exper-
ience for the invalid. But to sit aloft one's self
in the pure air and under the unclouded dome
of heaven, and thus look down on the submer-
gence of the valley, was strangely different and
even delightful to the eyes. Far away were hilltops like little islands. Nearer, a smoky surf
beat about the foot of precipices and poured into all the coves of these rough mountains. The
colour of that fog ocean was a thing never to
be forgotten. For an instant, among the Hebrides and just about sundown, I have seen some-

thing like it on the sea itself. But the white was not so opaline; nor was there, what surprisingly increased the effect, that breathless, crystal stillness over all. Even in its gentlest moods the salt sea travails, moaning among the weeds or lisping on the sand; but that vast fog ocean lay in a trance of silence, nor did the sweet air of the morning tremble with a sound.

As I continued to sit upon the dump, I began to observe that this sea was not so level as at first sight it appeared to be. Away in the extreme south, a little hill of fog arose against the sky above the general surface, and as it had already caught the sun, it shone on the horizon like the topsails of some giant ship. There were huge waves, stationary, as it seemed, like waves in a frozen sea; and yet, as I looked again, I was not sure but they were moving after all, with a slow and august advance. And while I was yet doubting, a promontory of the hills some four or five miles away, conspicuous by a bouquet of tall pines, was in a single instant overtaken and swallowed up. It reappeared in a little, with its pines, but this time as an islet, and only to be swallowed up once more and then for good. This set me looking nearer, and I saw that in every cove along the line of mountains the fog was being piled in higher and higher, as though by some wind that was inaudible to me. I could trace its progress, one pine tree first growing hazy and then disappearing after another; although sometimes there was none of this fore-running haze, but the whole opaque white ocean gave a start and swallowed a piece of mountain at a gulp. It was to flee these poisonous fogs that I had left the seaboard, and climbed so high among the mountains. And now, behold, here came the fog to besiege me in my chosen altitudes, and yet came so beautifully that my first thought was of welcome.

The sun had now gotten much higher, and through all the gaps of the hills it cast long bars of gold across that white ocean. An eagle, or some other very great bird of the mountain, came wheeling over the nearer pine-tops, and hung, poised and something sideways, as if to look abroad on that unwonted desolation, spying, perhaps with terror, for the eyries of her comrades. Then, with a long cry, she disappeared again towards Lake County and the clearer air. At length it seemed to me as if the flood were beginning to subside. The old landmarks, by whose disappearance I had measured its advance, here a crag, there a brave pine tree, now began, in the inverse order, to make their reappearance into daylight. I judged all danger of the fog was over. This was not Noah's flood; it was but a morning spring, and would now drift out seaward whence it came. So, mightily relieved, and a good deal exhilarated by the sight, I went into the house to light the fire.

I suppose it was nearly seven when I once more mounted the platform to look abroad. The fog ocean had swelled up enormously since last I saw it; and a few hundred feet below me, in the deep gap where the Toll House stands and the road runs through into Lake County, it had already topped the slope, and was pouring over and down the other side like driving smoke.

The Sea Fogs

The wind had climbed along with it; and though I was still in calm air, I could see the trees tossing below me, and their long, strident sighing mounted to me where I stood.

Half an hour later, the fog had surmounted all the ridge on the opposite side of the gap, though a shoulder of the mountain still warded it out of our canyon. Napa Valley and its bounding hills were now utterly blotted out. The fog, sunny white in the sunshine, was pouring over into Lake County in a huge, ragged cataract, tossing treetops appearing and disappearing in the spray. The air struck with a little chill, and set me coughing. It smelt strong of the fog, like the smell of a washing-house, but with a shrewd tang of the sea salt.

Had it not been for two things — the sheltering spur which answered as a dyke, and the great valley on the other side which rapidly engulfed whatever mounted — our own little platform in the canyon must have been already buried a hundred feet in salt and poisonous air. As it was, the interest of the scene entirely occupied our minds. We were set just out of the wind, and but just above the fog; we could listen to the voice of the one as to music on the stage; we could plunge our eyes down into the other, as into some flowing stream from over the parapet of a bridge; thus we looked on upon a strange, impetuous, silent, shifting exhibition of the powers of nature, and saw the familiar landscape changing from moment to moment like figures in a dream.

The imagination loves to trifle with what is not. Had this been indeed the deluge, I should have felt more strongly, but the emotion would have been similar in kind. I played with the idea, as the child flees in delighted terror from the creations of his fancy. The look of the thing helped me. And when at last I began to flee up the mountain, it was indeed partly to escape from the raw air that kept me coughing, but it was also part in play.

As I ascended the mountain-side, I came once more to overlook the upper surface of the fog; but it wore a different appearance from

what I had beheld at daybreak. For, first, the
sun now fell on it from high overhead, and its
surface shone and undulated like a great nor'-
land moor country, sheeted with untrodden
morning snow. And next the new level must
have been a thousand or fifteen hundred feet
higher than the old, so that only five or six
points of all the broken country below me still
stood out. Napa Valley was now one with Sonoma on the west. On the hither side, only a thin
scattered fringe of bluffs was unsubmerged;
and through all the gaps the fog was pouring
over, like an ocean, into the blue clear sunny
country on the east. There it was soon lost; for
it fell instantly into the bottom of the valleys,
following the water-shed; and the hilltops in
that quarter were still clear cut upon the eastern sky.

Through the Toll House gap and over the
near ridges on the other side, the deluge was
immense. A spray of thin vapour was thrown
high above it, rising and falling, and blown into fantastic shapes. The speed of its course was

like a mountain torrent. Here and there a few treetops were discovered and then whelmed again; and for one second, the bough of a dead pine beckoned out of the spray like the arm of a drowning man. But still the imagination was dissatisfied, still the ear waited for something more. Had this indeed been water (as it seemed so, to the eye), with what a plunge of reverberating thunder would it have rolled upon its course, disembowelling mountains and deracinating pines! And yet water it was, and seawater at that—true Pacific billows, only somewhat rarefied, rolling in mid-air among the hilltops.

I climbed still higher, among the red rattling gravel and dwarf underwood of Mount Saint Helena, until I could look right down upon Silverado, and admire the favoured nook in which it lay. The sunny plain of fog was several hundred feet higher; behind the protecting spur a gigantic accumulation of cottony vapour threatened with every second, to blow over and submerge our homestead; but the vortex setting past the Toll House was too strong; and there lay our little platform, in the arms of the deluge, but still enjoying its unbroken sunshine. About eleven, however, thin spray came flying over the friendly buttress, and I began to think the fog had hunted out its Jonah after all. But it was the last effort. The wind veered while we were at dinner, and began to blow squally from the mountain summit; and by half-past one, all that world of sea fogs was utterly routed and flying here and there into the south in little rags of cloud. And instead of a lone sea-beach, we found ourselves once more inhabiting a high mountain-side with the clear green country far below us, and the light smoke of Calistoga blowing in the air.

This was the great Russian campaign for that season. Now and then, in the early morning, a little white lakelet of fog would be seen far down in Napa Valley; but the heights were not again assailed, nor was the surrounding world again shut off from Silverado.

THE TOLL HOUSE

THE TOLL HOUSE, standing alone by the wayside under nodding pines, with its streamlet and water-tank; its backwoods, toll-bar, and well trodden croquet ground; the ostler standing by the stable door, chewing a straw; a glimpse of the Chinese cook in the back parts; and Mr. Hoddy in the bar, gravely alert and serviceable, and equally anxious to lend or borrow books;—dozed all day in the dusty sunshine, more than half asleep. There were no neighbours, except the Hansons up the hill. The traffic on the road was infinitesimal; only, at rare intervals, a couple in a waggon, or a dusty farmer on a spring-board, toiling over "the grade" to that metropolitan hamlet, Calistoga; and, at the fixed hours, the passage of the stages.

The nearest building was the school-house, down the road; and the school-ma'am boarded at the Toll House, walking thence in the morning to the little brown shanty, where she taught the young ones of the district, and returning thither pretty weary in the afternoon. She had chosen this outlying situation, I understood, for her health. Mr. Corwin was consumptive; so was Rufe; so was Mr. Jennings, the engineer. In short, the place was a kind of small Davos: consumptive folk consorting on a hilltop in the most unbroken idleness. Jennings never did anything that I could see, except now and then to fish, and generally to sit about in the bar and the verandah, waiting for something to happen. Corwin and Rufe did as little as possible; and if the school-ma'am, poor lady, had to work pretty hard all morning, she subsided when it was over into much the same dazed beatitude as all the rest.

Her special corner was the parlour—a very
genteel room, with Bible prints, a crayon portrait of Mrs. Corwin in the height of fashion,
a few years ago, another of her son (Mr. Corwin
was not represented), a mirror, and a selection
of dried grasses. A large book was laid religi-
ously on the table — "From Palace to Hovel,"
I believe its name—full of the raciest experiences
in England. The author had mingled freely
with all classes, the nobility particularly meet-
ing him with open arms; and I must say that
traveller had ill requited his reception. His book,
in short, was a capital instance of the Penny
Messalina school of literature; and there arose
from it, in that cool parlour, in that silent, wayside, mountain inn, a rank atmosphere of gold
and blood and "Jenkins," and the "Mysteries
of London," and sickening, inverted snobbery,
fit to knock you down. The mention of this book
reminds me of another and far racier picture of
our island life. The latter parts of *Rocambole* are
surely too sparingly consulted in the country
which they celebrate. No man's education can

be said to be complete, nor can he pronounce
the world yet emptied of enjoyment, till he has
made the acquaintance of "the Reverend Patterson, director of the Evangelical Society."
To follow the evolutions of that reverend gentleman, who goes through scenes in which even
Mr. Duffield would hesitate to place a bishop,
is to rise to new ideas. But, alas! there was no
Patterson about the Toll House. Only, alongside
of "From Palace to Hovel," a sixpenny "Ouida"
figured. So literature, you see, was not unrepre-
sented.

The school-ma'am had friends to stay with
her, other school-ma'ams enjoying their holi-
days, quite a bevy of damsels. They seemed
never to go out, or not beyond the verandah,
but sat close in the little parlour, quietly talking or listening to the wind among the trees.
Sleep dwelt in the Toll House, like a fixture:
summer sleep, shallow, soft, and dreamless. A
cuckoo-clock, a great rarity in such a place,
hooted at intervals about the echoing house;
and Mr. Jennings would open his eyes for a

moment in the bar, and turn the leaf of a newspaper, and the resting school-ma'ams in the
parlour would be recalled to the consciousness
of their inaction. Busy Mrs. Corwin and her
busy Chinaman might be heard indeed, in the
penetralia, pounding dough or rattling dishes;
or perhaps Rufe had called up some of the sleepers for a game of croquet, and the hollow strokes
of the mallet sounded far away among the
woods: but with these exceptions, it was sleep
and sunshine and dust, and the wind in the
pine trees, all day long.

A little before stage time, that castle of indo-
lence awoke. The ostler threw his straw away
and set to his preparations. Mr. Jennings rubbed
his eyes; happy Mr. Jennings, the something
he had been waiting for all day about to happen
at last! The boarders gathered in the verandah,
silently giving ear, and gazing down the road
with shaded eyes. And as yet there was no sign
for the senses, not a sound, not a tremor of the
mountain road. The birds, to whom the secret
of the hooting cuckoo is unknown, must have

set down to instinct this premonitory bustle.

And then the first of the two stages swooped upon the Toll House with a roar and in a cloud of dust; and the shock had not yet time to subside, before the second was abreast of it. Huge concerns they were, well-horsed and loaded, the men in their shirt-sleeves, the women swathed in veils, the long whip cracking like a pistol; and as they charged upon that slumbering hostelry, each shepherding a dust storm, the dead place blossomed into life and talk and clatter. This the Toll House? — with its city throng, its jostling shoulders, its infinity of instant business in the bar? The mind would not receive it! The heartfelt bustle of that hour is hardly credible; the thrill of the great shower of letters from the post-bag, the childish hope and interest with which one gazed in all these strangers' eyes. They paused there but to pass: the blue-clad China-boy, the San Francisco magnate, the mystery in the dust coat, the secret memoirs in tweed, the ogling well-shod lady with her troop of girls; they did but flash and go; they were hull-down for us behind life's ocean, and we but hailed their topsails on the line. Yet, out of our great solitude of four and twenty mountain hours, we thrilled to their momentary presence; gauged and divined them, loved and hated; and stood light-headed in that storm of human electricity. Yes, like Piccadilly Circus, this is also one of life's crossing-places. Here I beheld one man, already famous or infamous, a centre of pistol-shots: and another who, if not yet known to rumour, will fill a column of the Sunday paper when he comes to hang — a burly, thick-set, powerful Chinese desperado, six long bristles upon either lip; redolent of whiskey, playing cards, and pistols; swaggering in the bar with the lowest assumption of the lowest European manners; rapping out blackguard English oaths in his canorous oriental voice; and combining in one person the depravities of two races and two civilizations. For all his lust and vigour he seemed to look cold upon me from the valley of the shadow of the gallows. He imagined a vain thing; and

while he drained his cocktail, Holbein's death
was at his elbow. Once, too, I fell in talk with
another of these flitting strangers—like the rest,
in his shirt-sleeves and all begrimed with dust—
and the next minute we were discussing Paris
and London, theatres and wines. To him, jour-
neying from one human place to another, this
was a trifle; but to me! No, Mr. Lillie, I have
not forgotten it.

And presently the city-tide was at its flood and
began to ebb. Life runs in Piccadilly Circus, say,
from nine to one, and then, there also, ebbs into
the small hours of the echoing policeman and the
lamps and stars. But the Toll House is far up
stream, and near its rural springs; the bubble
of the tide but touches it. Before you had yet
grasped your pleasure, the horses were put to,
the loud whips volleyed, and the tide was gone.
North and south had the two stages vanished,
the towering dust subsided in the woods; but
there was still an interval before the flush had
fallen on your cheeks, before the ear became
once more contented with the silence, or the

seven sleepers of the Toll House dozed back to their accustomed corners. Yet a little, and the ostler would swing round the great barrier across the road; and in the golden evening, that dreamy inn begin to trim its lamps and spread the board for supper.

As I recall the place—the green dell below; the spires of pine; the sun-warm, scented air; that gray, gabled inn, with its faint stirrings of life amid the slumber of the mountains—I slowly awake to a sense of admiration, gratitude, and almost love. A fine place, after all, for a wasted life to doze away in—the cuckoo clock hooting of its far home country; the croquet mallets, eloquent of English lawns; the stages daily bringing news of the turbulent world away below there; and perhaps once in the summer, a salt fog pouring overhead with its tale of the Pacific.

A STARRY DRIVE

In our rule at Silverado, there was a melancholy interregnum. The queen and the crown prince with one accord fell sick; and, as I was sick to begin with, our lone position on Mount Saint Helena was no longer tenable, and we had to hurry back to Calistoga and a cottage on the green. By that time we had begun to realize the difficulties of our position. We had found what an amount of labour it cost to support life in our red canyon; and it was the dearest desire of our hearts to get a China-boy to go along with us when we returned. We could have given him a whole house to himself, self-contained, as they say in the advertisements; and on the money question we were prepared to go far. Kong Sam Kee, the Calistoga washerman, was entrusted with the affair; and from day to day it languished on, with protestations on our part and mellifluous excuses on the part of Kong Sam Kee.

At length, about half-past eight of our last evening, with the waggon ready harnessed to convey us up the grade, the washerman, with a somewhat sneering air, produced the boy. He was a handsome gentlemanly lad, attired in rich dark blue, and shod with snowy white; but, alas! he had heard rumours of Silverado. He knew it for a lone place on the mountain-side, with no friendly wash-house near by, where he might smoke a pipe of opium o' nights with other China-boys, and lose his little earnings at the game of tan; and he first backed out for more money; and then, when that demand was satisfied, refused to come point-blank. He was wedded to his wash-houses; he had no taste for the rural life; and we must go to our mountain servantless. It must have been near half an hour before we reached that conclusion, standing in the midst of Calistoga high street under the stars, and the China-boy and Kong Sam Kee singing their pigeon English in the sweetest voices and with the most musical inflections.

We were not, however, to return alone; for we brought with us Joe Strong, the painter, a most good-natured comrade and a capital hand at an omelette. I do not know in which capacity he was most valued—as a cook or a companion; and he did excellently well in both.

The Kong Sam Kee negociation had delayed us unduly; it must have been half-past nine before we left Calistoga, and night came fully ere we struck the bottom of the grade. I have never seen such a night. It seemed to throw calumny in the teeth of all the painters that ever dabbled in starlight. The sky itself was of a ruddy, powerful, nameless, changing colour, dark and glossy like a serpent's back. The stars, by innumerable millions, stuck boldly forth like lamps. The milky way was bright, like a moonlit cloud; half heaven seemed milky way. The

greater luminaries shone each more clearly than
a winter's moon. Their light was dyed in every
sort of colour — red, like fire; blue, like steel;
green, like the tracks of sunset; and so sharply
did each stand forth in its own lustre that there
was no appearance of that flat, star-spangled
arch we know so well in pictures, but all the
hollow of heaven was one chaos of contesting
luminaries — a hurly-burly of stars. Against
this the hills and rugged tree-tops stood out
redly dark.

As we continued to advance, the lesser lights
and milky ways first grew pale, and then vanished; the countless hosts of heaven dwindled
in number by successive millions; those that
still shone had tempered their exceeding brightness and fallen back into their customary wist-
ful distance; and the sky declined from its first
bewildering splendour into the appearance of a
common night. Slowly this change proceeded,
and still there was no sign of any cause. Then
a whiteness like mist was thrown over the spurs
of the mountain. Yet a while, and as we turned

a corner, a great leap of silver light and net of
forest shadows fell across the road and upon
our wondering waggonful; and, swimming low
among the trees, we beheld a strange, mis-
shapen, waning moon, half-tilted on her back.

"Where are ye when the moon appears?"
so the old poet sang, half-taunting, to the stars,
bent upon a courtly purpose.

> "*As the sunlight round the dim earth's*
>   *midnight tower of shadow pours,*
> *Streaming past the dim, wide portals,*
> *Viewless to the eyes of mortals,*
> *Till it floods the moon's pale islet or the*
>   *morning's golden shores.*"

So sings Mr. Trowbridge, with a noble inspir-
ation. And so had the sunlight flooded that pale
islet of the moon, and her lit face put out, one
after another, that galaxy of stars. The wonder
of the drive was over; but, by some nice conjunction of clearness in the air and fit shadow
in the valley where we travelled, we had seen
for a little while that brave display of the mid-

night heavens. It was gone, but it had been ;
nor shall I ever again behold the stars with the
same mind. He who has seen the sea commov-
ed with a great hurricane, thinks of it very
differently from him who has seen it only in a
calm. And the difference between a calm and a
hurricane is not greatly more striking than that
between the ordinary face of night and the
splendour that shone upon us in that drive.
Two in our waggon knew night as she shines
upon the tropics, but even that bore no com-
parison. The nameless colour of the sky, the
hues of the star-fire, and the incredible projec-
tion of the stars themselves, starting from their
orbits, so that the eye seemed to distinguish
their positions in the hollow of space — these
were things that we had never seen before and
shall never see again.

Meanwhile, in this altered night, we proceeded on our way among the scents and silence of the forest, reached the top of the grade,
wound up by Hanson's, and came at last to a
stand under the flying gargoyle of the chute.

A Starry Drive

Sam, who had been lying back, fast asleep, with the moon on his face, got down, with the remark that it was pleasant "to be home." The waggon turned and drove away, the noise gently dying in the woods, and we clambered up the rough path, Caliban's great feat of engineering, and came home to Silverado.

The moon shone in at the eastern doors and windows, and over the lumber on the platform. The one tall pine beside the ledge was steeped in silver. Away up the canyon, a wildcat welcomed us with three discordant squalls. But once we had lit a candle, and began to review our improvements, homely in either sense, and count our stores, it was wonderful what a feeling of possession and permanence grew up in the hearts of the lords of Silverado. A bed had still to be made up for Strong, and the morning's water to be fetched, with clinking pail; and as we set about these household duties, and showed off our wealth and conveniences before the stranger, and had a glass of wine, I think, in honour of our return, and trooped at length one after another up the flying bridge of plank, and lay down to sleep in our shattered, moon-pierced barrack, we were among the happiest sovereigns in the world, and certainly ruled over the most contented people. Yet, in our absence, the palace had been sacked. Wild cats, so the Hansons said, had broken in and carried off a side of bacon, a hatchet, and two knives.

EPISODES
IN THE
STORY OF A MINE

NO ONE could live at Silverado and not be
curious about the story of the mine. We were
surrounded by so many evidences of expense
and toil, we lived so entirely in the wreck of that
great enterprise, like mites in the ruins of a
cheese, that the idea of the old din and bustle
haunted our repose. Our own house, the forge,
the dump, the chutes, the rails, the windlass,
the mass of broken plant; the two tunnels, one
far below in the green dell, the other on the platform where we kept our wine; the deep shaft,
with the sun-glints and the water-drops; above
all, the ledge, that great gaping slice out of the

mountain shoulder, propped apart by wooden
wedges, on whose immediate margin, high
above our heads, the one tall pine precariously
nodded—these stood for its greatness; while,
the dog-hutch, boot-jacks, old boots, old tavern
bills, and the very beds that we inherited from
bygone miners, put in human touches and re-
alized for us the story of the past.

I have sat on an old sleeper, under the thick
madronas near the forge, with just a look over
the dump on the green world below, and seen
the sun lying broad among the wreck, and
heard the silence broken only by the tinkling
water in the shaft, or a stir of the royal family
about the battered palace, and my mind has
gone back to the epoch of the Stanleys and the
Chapmans with a grand *tutti* of pick and drill,
hammer and anvil, echoing about the canyon;
the assayer hard at it in our dining-room; the
carts below on the road, and their cargo of red
mineral bounding and thundering down the
iron chute. And now all gone—all fallen away
into this sunny silence and desertion: a family

of squatters dining in the assayer's office, making their beds in the big sleeping room erstwhile so crowded, keeping their wine in the tunnel that once rang with picks.

But Silverado itself, although now fallen in its turn into decay, was once but a mushroom, and had succeeded to other mines and other flitting cities. Twenty years ago, away down the glen on the Lake County side there was a place, Jonestown by name, with two thousand inhabitants dwelling under canvas, and one roofed house for the sale of whiskey. Round on the western side of Mount Saint Helena, there was at the same date, a second large encampment, its name, if it ever had one, lost for me. Both of these have perished, leaving not a stick and scarce a memory behind them. Tide after tide of hopeful miners have thus flowed and ebbed about the mountain, coming and going, now by lone prospectors, now with a rush. Last, in order of time came Silverado, reared the big mill, in the valley, founded the town which is now represented, monumentally, by Hanson's, pierced all these slaps and shafts and tunnels, and in turn declined and died away.

"Our noisy years seem moments in the wake
Of the eternal silence."

As to the success of Silverado in its time of being, two reports were current. According to the first, six hundred thousand dollars were taken out of that great upright seam, that still hung open above us on crazy wedges. Then the ledge pinched out, and there followed, in quest of the remainder, a great drifting and tunnelling in all directions, and a great consequent effusion of dollars, until, all parties being sick of the expense, the mine was deserted, and the town decamped. According to the second version, told me with much secrecy of manner, the whole affair, mine, mill, and town, were parts of one majestic swindle. There had never come any silver out of any portion of the mine; there was no silver to come. At midnight trains of packhorses might have been observed winding by devious tracks about the shoulder of the mountain. They came from far away, from Amador or Placer, laden with silver in "old cigar boxes." They discharged their load at Silverado, in the hour of sleep; and before the morning they were gone again with their mysterious drivers to their unknown source. In this way, twenty thousand pounds' worth of silver was smuggled in under cover of night, in these old cigar boxes; mixed with Silverado mineral; carted down to the mill; crushed, amalgated, and refined, and despatched to the city as the proper product of the mine. Stock-jobbing, if it can cover such expenses, must be a profitable business in San Francisco.

I give these two versions as I got them. But I place little reliance on either, my belief in history having been greatly shaken. For it chanced that I had come to dwell in Silverado at a critical hour; great events in its history were about to happen—did happen, as I am led to believe; nay, and it will be seen that I played a part in that revolution myself. And yet from first to last I never had a glimmer of an idea what was going on; and even now, after full reflection, profess myself at sea. That there was some obscure intrigue of the cigar-box order, and that I, in the character of a wooden puppet, set pen to paper in the interest of somebody, so much, and no more, is certain.

Silverado, then under my immediate sway, belonged to one whom I will call a Mr. Ronalds. I only knew him through the extraordinarily distorting medium of local gossip, now as a momentous jobber; now as a dupe to point an adage; and again, and much more probably, as an ordinary Christian gentleman like you or me, who had opened a mine and worked it for a while with better and worse fortune. So, through a defective window-pane, you may see the passerby shoot up into a hunchbacked giant or dwindle into a potbellied dwarf.

To Ronalds, at least, the mine belonged; but the notice by which he held it would run out upon the 30th of June—or rather, as I suppose, it had run out already, and the month of grace would expire upon that day, after which any

American citizen might post a notice of his own, and make Silverado his. This, with a sort of quiet slyness, Rufe told me at an early period of our acquaintance. There was no silver, of course; the mine "wasn't worth nothing, Mr. Stevens," but there was a deal of old iron and wood around, and to gain possession of this old wood and iron, and get a right to the water, Rufe proposed, if I had no objections, to "jump the claim."

Of course, I had no objection. But I was filled with wonder. If all he wanted was the wood and iron, what, in the name of fortune, was to prevent him taking them? "His right there was none to dispute." He might lay hands on all tomorrow, as the wild cats had laid hands upon our knives and hatchet. Besides, was this mass of heavy mining plant worth transportation? If it was why had not the rightful owners carted it away? If it was, would they not preserve their title to these movables, even after they had lost their title to the mine? And if it were not, what the better was Rufe? Nothing would grow at

Silverado; there was even no wood to cut; beyond a sense of property, there was nothing to be gained. Lastly, was it at all credible that Ronalds would forget what Rufe remembered? The days of grace were not yet over: any fine morning he might appear, paper in hand, and enter for another year on his inheritance. However, it was none of my business; all seemed legal; Rufe or Ronalds, all was one to me.

On the morning of the 27th, Mrs. Hanson appeared with the milk as usual, in her sunbonnet. The time would be out on Tuesday, she reminded us, and bade me be in readiness to play my part, though I had no idea what it was to be. And suppose Ronalds came? we asked. She received the idea with derision, laughing aloud with all her fine teeth. He could not find the mine to save his life, it appeared, without Rufe to guide him. Last year, when he came, they heard him "up and down the road a hollerin' and a raisin' Cain." And at last he had to come to the Hansons in despair, and bid Rufe, "Jump into your pants and shoes, and show me

where this old mine is, anyway!" Seeing that
Ronalds had laid out so much money in the spot,
and that a beaten road led right up to the bottom of the dump, I thought this a remarkable
example. The sense of locality must be singularly in abeyance in the case of Ronalds.

That same evening, supper comfortably over,
Joe Strong busy at work on a drawing of the
dump and the opposite hills, we were all out on
the platform together, sitting there, under the
tented heavens, with the same sense of privacy
as if we had been cabined in a parlour, when
the sound of brisk footsteps came mounting up
the path. We pricked our ears at this, for the
tread seemed lighter and firmer than was usual
with our country neighbours. And presently,
sure enough, two town gentlemen, with cigars
and kid gloves, came debouching past the house.
They looked in that place like a blasphemy.

"Good evening," they said. For none of us
had stirred; we all sat stiff with wonder.

"Good evening," I returned; and then, to put
them at their ease, "A stiff climb," I added.

throw myself on my knees and own the intended treachery. But then I had Hanson to consider. I was in much the same position as Old Rowley, that royal humourist, whom "the rogue had taken into his confidence." And again, here was Ronalds on the spot. He must know the day of the month as well as Hanson and I. If a broad hint were necessary, he had the broadest in the world. For a large board had been nailed by the crown prince on the very front of our house, between the door and window, painted in cinnabar—the pigment of the country—with doggrel rhymes and contumelious pictures, and announcing, in terms unnecessarily figurative, that the trick was already played, the claim already jumped, and Master Sam the legitimate successor of Mr. Ronalds. But no, nothing could save that man; *quem deus vult perdere, prius dementat.* As he came so he went, and left his rights depending. Late at night, by Silverado reckoning, and after we were all abed, Mrs. Hanson returned to give us the newest of her news. It was like a scene in a ship's steerage:

all of us abed in our different tiers, the single candle struggling with the darkness, and this plump, handsome woman, seated on an upturned valise beside the bunks, talking and showing her fine teeth, and laughing till the rafters rang. Any ship, to be sure, with a hundredth part as many holes in it as our barrack, must long ago have gone to her last port. Up to that time I had always imagined Mrs. Hanson's loquacity to be mere incontinence, that she said what was uppermost for the pleasure of speaking, and laughed and laughed again as a kind of musical accompaniment. But I now found there was an art in it. I found it less communicative than silence itself. I wished to know why Ronalds had come; how he had found his way without Rufe; and why, being on the spot, he had not refreshed his title. She talked interminably on, but her replies were never answers. She fled under a cloud of words; and when I had made sure that she was purposely eluding me, I dropped the subject in my turn, and let her rattle where she would.

She had come to tell us that, instead of waiting for Tuesday, the claim was to be jumped
on the morrow. How? If the time were not out,
it was impossible. Why? If Ronalds had come
and gone, and done nothing, there was the less
cause for hurry. But again I could reach no
satisfaction. The claim was to be jumped next
morning, that was all that she would conde-
scend upon.

And yet it was not jumped the next morning,
nor yet the next, and a whole week had come
and gone before we heard more of this exploit.
That day week, however, a day of great heat,
Hanson, with a little roll of paper in his hand,
and the eternal pipe alight; Breedlove, his large,
dull friend, to act, I suppose, as witness; Mrs.
Hanson, in her Sunday best; and all the children, from the oldest to the youngest;—arrived in
a procession, tailing one behind another up the
path. Caliban was absent, but he had been chary
of his friendly visits since the row; and with that
exception, the whole family was gathered together as for a marriage or a christening. Strong

was sitting at work, in the shade of the dwarf madronas near the forge; and they planted themselves about him in a circle, one on a stone, another on the waggon rails, a third on a piece of plank. Gradually the children stole away up the canyon to where there was another chute, somewhat smaller than the one across the dump; and down this chute, for the rest of the afternoon, they poured one avalanche of stones after another, waking the echoes of the glen. Meantime we elders sat together on the platform, Hanson and his friend smoking in silence like Indian sachems, Mrs. Hanson rattling on as usual with an adroit volubility, saying nothing, but keeping the party at their ease like a courtly hostess.

Not a word occurred about the business of the day. Once, twice, and thrice I tried to slide the subject in, but was discouraged by the stoic apathy of Rufe, and beaten down before the pouring verbiage of his wife. There is nothing of the Indian brave about me, and I began to grill with impatience. At last, like a highway robber, I cornered Hanson, and bade him stand

and deliver his business. Thereupon he gravely
rose, as though to hint that this was not a proper place, nor the subject one suitable for squaws,
and I, following his example, led him up the
plank into our barrack. There he bestowed himself on a box, and unrolled his papers with fas-
tidious deliberation. There were two sheets of
note-paper, and an old mining notice, dated
May 30th, 1879, part print, part manuscript,
and the latter much obliterated by the rains. It
was by this identical piece of paper that the
mine had been held last year. For thirteen
months it had endured the weather and the
change of seasons on a cairn behind the shoulder of the canyon; and it was now my business,
spreading it before me on the table, and sitting
on a valise, to copy its terms, with some necessary changes, twice over on the two sheets of
note-paper. One was then to be placed on the
same cairn—a "mound of rocks" the notice put
it; and the other to be lodged for registration.

Rufe watched me, silently smoking, till I came
to the place for the locator's name at the end of

the first copy; and when I proposed that he should sign, I thought I saw a scare in his eye. "I don't think that'll be necessary," he said slowly; "just you write it down." Perhaps this mighty hunter, who was the most active member of the local school board, could not write. There would be nothing strange in that. The constable of Calistoga is, and has been for years, a bed-ridden man, and, if I remember rightly, blind. He had more need of the emoluments than another, it was explained; and it was easy for him to "depytize," with a strong accent on the last. So friendly and so free are popular institutions.

When I had done my scrivening, Hanson strolled out, and addressed Breedlove, "Will you step up here a bit?" and after they had disappeared a little while into the chaparral and madrona thicket, they came back again, minus a notice, and the deed was done. The claim was jumped; a tract of mountain-side, fifteen hundred feet long by six hundred wide, with all the earth's precious bowels, had passed from Ron-

alds to Hanson, and, in the passage, changed
its name from the "Mammoth" to the "Calistoga." I had tried to get Rufe to call it after his
wife, after himself, and after Garfield, the Re-
publican presidential candidate of the hour —
since then elected, and, alas! dead—but all was
in vain. The claim had once been called the
Calistoga before, and he seemed to feel safety
in returning to that.

And so the history of that mine became once
more plunged in darkness, lit only by some
monster pyrotechnical displays of gossip. And
perhaps the most curious feature of the whole
matter is this: that we should have dwelt in this
quiet corner of the mountains, with not a dozen
neighbours, and yet struggled all the while, like
desperate swimmers, in this sea of falsities and
contradictions. Wherever a man is, there will
be a lie.

Toils and Pleasures

I must try to convey some notion of our life, of how the days passed and what pleasure we took in them, of what there was to do and how we set about doing it, in our mountain hermitage. The house, after we had repaired the worst of the damages, and filled in some of the doors and windows with white cotton cloth, became a healthy and a pleasant dwelling-place, always airy and dry, and haunted by the outdoor perfumes of the glen. Within, it had the look of habitation, the human look. You had only to go into the third room, which we did not use, and see its stones, its sifting earth, its tumbled litter; and then return to our lodging, with the beds made, the plates on the rack, the pail of bright water behind the door, the stove crackling in a corner, and perhaps the table roughly laid against a meal,—and man's order, the little clean spots that he creates to dwell in, were at once contrasted with the rich passivity of nature. And yet our house was everywhere so wrecked and shattered, the air came and went so freely, the sun found so many portholes, the golden outdoor glow shone in so many open chinks, that we enjoyed, at the same time, some of the comforts of a roof and much of the gaiety and brightness of al fresco life. A single shower of rain, to be sure, and we should have been drowned out like mice. But ours was a Californian summer, and an earthquake was a far likelier accident than a shower of rain.

Trustful in this fine weather, we kept the house for kitchen and bedroom, and used the platform as our summer parlour. The sense of privacy, as I have said already, was complete. We could look over the dump on miles of forest

and rough hilltop; our eyes commanded some of
Napa Valley, where the train ran, and the little
country townships sat so close together along
the line of the rail. But here there was no man
to intrude. None but the Hansons were our visitors. Even they came but at long intervals, or
twice daily, at a stated hour, with milk. So our
days, as they were never interrupted, drew out
to the greater length; hour melted insensibly into hour; the household duties, though they were
many, and some of them laborious, dwindled
into mere islets of business in a sea of sunny
day-time; and it appears to me, looking back,
as though the far greater part of our life at Silverado had been passed, propped upon an elbow, or seated on a plank, listening to the silence that there is among the hills.

My work, it is true, was over early in the
morning. I rose before any one else, lit the
stove, put on the water to boil, and strolled
forth upon the platform to wait till it was ready.
Silverado would then be still in shadow, the
sun shining on the mountain higher up. A clean

smell of trees, a smell of the earth at morning, hung in the air. Regularly, every day, there was a single bird, not singing, but awkwardly chirruping among the green madronas, and the sound was cheerful, natural, and stirring. It did not hold the attention, nor interrupt the thread of meditation, like a blackbird or a nightingale; it was mere woodland prattle, of which the mind was conscious like a perfume. The freshness of these morning seasons remained with me far on into the day.

As soon as the kettle boiled, I made porridge and coffee; and that, beyond the literal drawing of water, and the preparation of kindling, which it would be hyperbolical to call the hewing of wood, ended my domestic duties for the day. Thenceforth my wife laboured single-handed in the palace, and I lay or wandered on the platform at my own sweet will. The little corner near the forge, where we found a refuge under the madronas from the unsparing early sun, is indeed connected in my mind with some nightmare encounters over Euclid, and the Latin

Toils and Pleasures

Grammar. These were known as Sam's lessons. He was supposed to be the victim and the sufferer; but here there must have been some misconception, for whereas I generally retired to bed after one of these engagements, he was no sooner set free than he dashed up to the Chinaman's house, where he had installed a printing press, that great element of civilization, and the sound of his labours would be faintly audible about the canyon half the day.

To walk at all was a laborious business; the foot sank and slid, the boots were cut to pieces, among sharp, uneven, rolling stones. When we crossed the platform in any direction, it was usual to lay a course, following as much as possible the line of waggon rails. Thus, if water were to be drawn, the water-carrier left the house along some tilting planks that we had laid down, and not laid down very well. These carried him to that great highroad, the railway; and the railway served him as far as to the head of the shaft. But from thence to the spring and back again he made the best of his unaided way, staggering among the stones, and wading in low growth of the calcanthus, where the rattlesnakes lay hissing at his passage. Yet I liked to draw water. It was pleasant to dip the gray metal pail into the clean, colourless, cool water; pleasant to carry it back, with the water lipping at the edge, and a broken sunbeam quivering in the midst.

But the extreme roughness of the walking confined us in common practice to the platform, and indeed to those parts of it that were most easily accessible along the line of rails. The rails came straight forward from the shaft, here and there overgrown with little green bushes, but still entire, and still carrying a truck, which it was Sam's delight to trundle to and fro by the hour with various ladings. About midway down the platform, the railroad trended to the right, leaving our house and coasting along the far side within a few yards of the madronas and the forge, and not far off the latter, ended in a sort of platform on the edge of the dump. There, in old days, the trucks were tipped, and their load sent thundering down the chute. There, besides, was the only spot where we could approach the margin of the dump. Anywhere else, you took your life in your right hand when you came within a yard and a half to peer over. For at any moment the dump might begin to slide and carry you down and bury you below its ruins. Indeed, the neighbourhood of an old mine is a place beset with dangers. For as still as Silverado was, at any moment the report of rotten wood might tell us that the platform had fallen into the shaft; the dump might begin to pour into the road below; or a wedge slip in the great upright seam, and hundreds of tons of mountain bury the scene of our encampment.

I have already compared the dump to a rampart, built certainly by some rude people, and for prehistoric wars. It was likewise a frontier. All below was green and woodland, the tall pines soaring one above another, each with a firm outline and full spread of bough. All above was arid, rocky, and bald. The great spout of broken mineral, that had dammed the canyon up, was a creature of man's handiwork, its material dug out with a pick and powder, and spread by the service of the trucks. But nature herself, in that upper district, seemed to have had an eye to nothing besides mining; and even the natural hillside was all sliding gravel and precarious boulder. Close at the margin of the well leaves would decay to skeletons and mummies, which at length some stronger gust would carry clear of the canyon and scatter in the subjacent woods. Even moisture and decaying vegetable matter could not, with all nature's alchemy, concoct enough soil to nourish a few poor grasses. It is the same, they say, in the neighbourhood of all silver mines; the nature of that precious rock being stubborn with quartz and poisonous with cinnabar. Both were plenty in our Silverado. The stones sparkled white in the sunshine with quartz; they were all stained red with cinnabar. Here, doubtless, came the Indians of yore to paint their faces for the warpath; and cinnabar, if I remember rightly, was one of the few articles of Indian commerce.

Toils and Pleasures

Now, Sam had it in his undisturbed possession, to pound down and slake, and paint his rude designs with. But to me it had always a fine flavour of poetry, compounded out of Indian story and Hawthornden's allusion:

"*Desire, alas! desire a Zeuxis new,*
From Indies borrowing gold, from Eastern skies,
Most bright cinoper . . . "

Yet this is but half the picture; our Silverado platform has another side to it. Though there was no soil, and scarce a blade of grass, yet out of these tumbled gravel-heaps and broken boulders, a flower garden bloomed as at home in a conservatory. Calcanthus crept, like a hardy weed, all over our rough parlour, choking the railway, and pushing forth its rusty, aromatic cones from between two blocks of shattered mineral. Azaleas made a big snow-bed just above the well. The shoulder of the hill waved white with Mediterranean heath. In the crannies of the ledge and about the spurs of the tall pine, a red flowering stone-plant hung in clus-

ters. Even the low, thorny chaparral was thick
with pea-like blossom. Close at the foot of our
path nutmegs prospered, delightful to the sight
and smell. At sunrise, and again late at night,
the scent of the sweet bay trees filled the canyon, and the down-blowing night wind must
have borne it hundreds of feet into the outer air.

All this vegetation, to be sure, was stunted.
The madrona was here no bigger than the manzanita; the bay was but a stripling shrub; the
very pines, with four or five exceptions in all our
upper canyon, were not so tall as myself, or but
a little taller, and the most of them came lower
than my waist. For a prosperous forest tree, we
must look below, where the glen was crowded
with green spires. But for flowers and ravish-
ing perfume, we had none to envy; our heap of
road-metal was thick with bloom, like a hawthorn in the front of June; our red, baking angle
in the mountain, a laboratory of poignant scents.
It was an endless wonder to my mind, as I
dreamed about the platform, following the progress of the shadows, where the madrona with

its leaves, the azalea and calcanthus with their blossoms, could find moisture to support such thick, wet, waxy growths, or the bay tree collect the ingredients of its perfume. But there they all grew together, healthy, happy, and happy-making, as though rooted in a fathom of black soil.

Nor was it only vegetable life that prospered. We had, indeed, few birds, and none that had much of a voice or anything worthy to be called a song. My morning comrade had a thin chirp, unmusical and monotonous, but friendly and pleasant to hear. He had but one rival; a fellow with an ostentatious cry of near an octave descending, not one note of which properly followed another. This is the only bird I ever knew with a wrong ear; but there was something enthralling about his performance. You listened and listened, thinking each time he must surely get it right; but no, it was always wrong, and always wrong the same way. Yet he seemed proud of his song, delivered it with execution and a manner of his own, and was charming to his mate. A very incorrect, incessant human whistler had thus a chance of knowing how his own music pleased the world. Two great birds — eagles, we thought—dwelt at the top of the canyon, among the crags that were printed on the sky. Now and again, but very rarely, they wheeled high over our heads in silence, or with a distant, dying scream; and then, with a fresh impulse, winged fleetly forward, dipped over a hilltop, and were gone. They seemed solemn and ancient things, sailing the blue air: perhaps co-œval with the mountain where they haunted, perhaps emigrants from Rome, where the glad legions may have shouted to behold them on the morn of battle.

But if the birds were rare, the place abounded with rattlesnakes — the rattlesnake's nest, it might have been named. Wherever we brushed among the bushes, our passage woke their angry buzz. One dwelt habitually in the wood-pile, and sometimes, when we came for firewood, thrust up his small head between two logs, and hissed at the intrusion. The rattle has a legendary credit; it is said to be awe-inspiring, and, once heard, to stamp itself for ever in the memory. But the sound is not at all alarming; the hum of many insects, and the buzz of the wasp convince the ear of danger quite as readily. As a matter of fact, we lived for weeks in Silverado, coming and going, with rattles sprung on every side, and it never occurred to us to be afraid. I used to take sun-baths and do calisthenics in a certain pleasant nook among azalea and calcanthus, the rattles whizzing on every side like spinning-wheels, and the combined hiss or buzz rising louder and angrier at any sudden movement; but I was never in the least impressed, nor ever attacked. It was only towards the end of our stay, that a man down at Calistoga, who was expatiating on the terrifying nature of the sound, gave me at last a very good imitation; and it burst on me at once that we dwelt in the very metropolis of deadly snakes, and that the rattle was simply the commonest noise in Silverado. Immediately on our return, we attacked the Hansons on the subject. They

had formerly assured us that our canyon was
favoured, like Ireland, with an entire immunity
from poisonous reptiles; but, with the perfect
inconsequence of the natural man, they were
no sooner found out than they went off at score
in the contrary direction, and we were told that
in no part of the world did rattlesnakes attain to
such a monstrous bigness as among the warm,
flower-dotted rocks of Silverado. This is a con-
tribution rather to the natural history of the
Hansons, than to that of snakes.

One person, however, better served by his
instinct, had known the rattle from the first;
and that was Chuchu, the dog. No rational creature has ever led an existence more poisoned by
terror than that dog's at Silverado. Every whiz
of the rattle made him bound. His eyes rolled;
he trembled; he would be often wet with sweat.
One of our great mysteries was his terror of the
mountain. A little away above our nook, the
azaleas and almost all the vegetation ceased.
Dwarf pines not big enough to be Christmas
trees, grew thinly among loose stone and grav-

el scaurs. Here and there a big boulder sat qui-
escent on a knoll, having paused there till the
next rain in his long slide down the mountain.
There was here no ambuscade for the snakes,
you could see clearly where you trod; and yet
the higher I went, the more abject and appealing became Chuchu's terror. He was an excellent master of that composite language in which
dogs communicate with men, and he would assure me, on his honour, that there was some
peril on the mountain; appeal to me, by all that
I held holy, to turn back; and at length, finding
all was in vain, and that I still persisted, ignor-
antly foolhardy, he would suddenly whip round
and make a bee-line down the slope for Silverado, the gravel showering after him. What was
he afraid of? There were admittedly brown
bears and California lions on the mountain; and
a grizzly visited Rufe's poultry yard not long
before, to the unspeakable alarm of Caliban,
who dashed out to chastise the intruder, and
found himself, by moonlight, face to face with
such a tartar. Something at least there must

have been: some hairy, dangerous brute lodged permanently among the rocks a little to the northwest of Silverado, spending his summer thereabout with his wife and family.

And there was, or there had been, another animal. Once, under the broad daylight, on that open stony hillside, where the baby pines were growing, scarcely tall enough to be a badge for a MacGregor's bonnet, I came suddenly upon his innocent body, lying mummified by the dry air and sun: a pigmy kangaroo. I am ingloriously ignorant of these subjects; had never heard of such a beast; thought myself face to face with some incomparable sport of nature; and began to cherish hopes of immortality in science. Rarely have I been conscious of a stranger thrill than when I raised that singular creature from the stones, dry as a board, his innocent heart long quiet, and all warm with sunshine. His long hind legs were stiff, his tiny forepaws clutched upon his breast, as if to leap; his poor life cut short upon that mountain by some unknown accident. But the kangaroo rat, it proved, was no such unknown animal; and my discovery was nothing.

Crickets were not wanting. I thought I could make out exactly four of them, each with a corner of his own, who used to make night musical at Silverado. In the matter of voice, they far excelled the birds, and their ringing whistle sounded from rock to rock, calling and replying the same thing, as in a meaningless opera. Thus, children in full health and spirits shout together, to the dismay of neighbours; and their idle, happy, deafening vociferations rise and fall, like the song of the crickets. I used to sit at night on the platform, and wonder why these creatures were so happy; and what was wrong with man that he also did not wind up his days with an hour or two of shouting; but I suspect that all long-lived animals are solemn. The dogs alone are hardly used by nature; and it seems a manifest injustice for poor Chuchu to die in his teens, after a life so shadowed and troubled, continually shaken with alarm, and the tear of elegant sentiment permanently in his eye.

There was another neighbour of ours at Silverado, small but very active, a destructive fellow. This was a black, ugly fly — a bore, the Hansons called him — who lived by hundreds in the boarding of our house. He entered by a round hole, more neatly pierced than a man could do it with a gimlet, and he seems to have spent his life in cutting out the interior of the plank, but whether as a dwelling or a storehouse, I could never find. When I used to lie in bed in the morning for a rest — we had no easy-chairs in Silverado — I would hear, hour after hour, the sharp cutting sound of his labours, and from time to time a dainty shower of sawdust would fall upon the blankets. There lives no more industrious creature than a bore.

And now that I have named to the reader all our animals and insects without exception — only I find I have forgotten the flies — he will be able to appreciate the singular privacy and silence of our days. It was not only man who was excluded: animals, the song of birds, the lowing of cattle, the bleating of sheep, clouds even,

and the variations of the weather, were here
also wanting; and as day after day, the sky was
one dome of blue, and the pines below us stood
motionless in the still air, so the hours themselves were marked out from each other only
by the series of our own affairs, and the sun's
great period as he ranged westward through
the heavens. The two birds cackled a while in
the early morning; all day the water tinkled in
the shaft, the bores ground sawdust in the
planking of our crazy palace — infinitesimal
sounds; and it was only with the return of night
that any change would fall on our surroundings,
or the four crickets begin to flute together in
the dark.

Indeed, it would be hard to exaggerate the
pleasure that we took in the approach of evening. Our day was not very long, but it was very
tiring. To trip along unsteady planks or wade
among shifting stones, to go to and fro for water, to clamber down the glen to the Toll House
after meat and letters, to cook, to make fires and
beds, were all exhausting to the body. Life out

of doors, besides, under the fierce eye of day, draws largely on the animal spirits. There are certain hours in the afternoon when a man, unless he is in strong health or enjoys a vacant mind, would rather creep into a cool corner of a house and sit upon the chairs of civilization. About that time, the sharp stones, the planks, the upturned boxes of Silverado, began to grow irksome to my body; I set out on that hopeless, never-ending quest for a more comfortable posture; I would be fevered and weary of the staring sun; and just then he would begin courteously to withdraw his countenance, the shadows lengthened, the aromatic airs awoke, and an indescribable but happy change announced the coming of the night.

The hours of evening, when we were once curtained in the friendly dark, sped lightly. Even as with the crickets, night brought to us a certain spirit of rejoicing. It was good to taste the air; good to mark the dawning of the stars, as they increased their glittering company; good, too, to gather stones, and send them crash-

ing down the chute, a wave of light. It seemed,
in some way, the reward and the fulfillment of
the day. So it is when men dwell in the open
air; it is one of the simple pleasures that we lose
by living cribbed and covered in a house, that,
though the coming of the day is still the most
inspiriting, yet day's departure, also, and the
return of night refresh, renew, and quiet us;
and in the pastures of the dusk we stand, like
cattle, exulting in the absence of the load.

Our nights were never cold, and they were
always still, but for one remarkable exception,
Regularly, about nine o'clock, a warm wind
sprang up, and blew for ten minutes, or maybe
a quarter of an hour, right down the canyon,
fanning it well out, airing it as a mother airs
the night nursery before the children sleep. As
far as I could judge, in the clear darkness of the
night, this wind was purely local: perhaps de-
pendent on the configuration of the glen. At
least, it was very welcome to the hot and weary
squatters; and if we were not abed already, the
springing up of this lilliputian valley-wind

would often be our signal to retire.

I was the last to go to bed, as I was still the first to rise. Many a night I have strolled about the platform, taking a bath of darkness before I slept. The rest would be in bed, and even from the forge I could hear them talking together from bunk to bunk. A single candle in the neck of a pint bottle was their only illumination; and yet the old cracked house seemed literally bursting with the light. It shone keen as a knife through all the vertical chinks; it struck upward through the broken shingles; and through the eastern door and window, it fell in a great splash upon the thicket and the overhanging rock. You would have said a conflagration, or at least a roaring forge; and behold, it was but a candle. Or perhaps it was yet more strange to see the procession moving bedwards round the corner of the house, and up the plank that brought us to the bedroom door; under the immense spread of the starry heavens, down in a crevice of the giant mountain, these few human shapes, with their unshielded taper, made so

disproportionate a figure in the eye and mind.
But the more he is alone with nature, the greater man and his doings bulk in the consideration
of his fellow-men. Miles and miles away upon
the opposite hilltops, if there were any hunter
belated or any traveller who had lost his way,
he must have stood, and watched and wondered,
from the time the candle issued from the door
of the assayer's office till it had mounted the
plank and disappeared again into the miners'
dormitory.

PRINTED AT THE GRABHORN PRESS

SAN FRANCISCO

Beobook
31